WHY WOULD ANYONE JOIN THE MORMON CHURCH?

WHY WOULD
ANYONE JOIN THE
MORMON
CHURCH?

BRAD BRASE

ISBN: 1-55517-387-1

v.5

Published by: **Bonneville Books**
Distributed by:
925 North Main, Springville, UT 84663 • 801/489-4084

CFI
Publishing and
Distribution Since 1986

Cedar Fort, Incorporated
CFI Distribution • CFI Books • Council Press • Bonneville Books

Cover Design by Corinne A. Bischoff
Lithographed in the United States of America

TABLE OF CONTENTS

WHY WOULD ANYONE JOIN THE MORMON CHURCH?

It is by now common knowledge among most of my friends, relatives, and associates, that I have joined The Church of Jesus Christ of Latter-day Saints, otherwise known as the Mormon Church. Having been raised in a Protestant home, my baptism into the LDS (Latter-day Saint) Church was quite a surprise, to say the least, to most who know me. Many thought, or even hoped, that this would only be a frivolous phase through which I would soon pass, yet time has only managed to strengthen my faith and substantiate the seriousness and sincerity of my personal convictions.

Knowing that many questions were left unanswered at the time of my conversion relative to my decision to join the LDS Church, I have taken it upon myself to discuss a few, but by no means all, of the reasons for my affiliation with the Latter-day Saints. In this book — which started years ago as nothing more than a personal letter to close family members and friends — I hope to clearly present some of the basic teachings of the LDS Church that influenced me during my prayerful investigation into the Church, and which inevitably led me to the conclusion that the gospel taught by the Latter-day Saints is the same gospel that was taught by the Savior and his apostles almost 2,000 years ago.

In presenting these gospel principles, I hope to foster a spirit of tolerance, unity, and understanding between Latter-day Saints and others in the Christian community. My intent is not to convince others of my beliefs, for that would be impossible. Only the Spirit of the Lord can bring man to a knowledge of the truth. Rather, I hope to inform, for it has been my experience that most people outside of the LDS Church possess a very inaccurate picture of LDS beliefs and practices. I offer this message in the true spirit of brotherly love, desiring to offend no one, and harboring only the kindest of feelings toward those whose prerogative it is to believe differently than me.

Many people have wondered, with the myriad Christian denominations in existence today, why I would abandon my Protestant beliefs in order to identify myself with a church as unpopular as the LDS Church. In fact, a good-intentioned instructor from a local Protestant college once commented to me that he couldn't understand "why anyone would want to belong to the Mormon Church." Through further discussion, I soon discovered the real cause of his confusion. He had a very distorted perspective of the Church and a gross misunderstanding of its true teachings. If my knowledge of the Church was as limited and erroneous as his, I, too, would share in his bewilderment.

I have come to realize that such widespread misunderstandings are the result of an information gap. It seems that a dichotomy of information exists concerning the LDS Church. On one hand, there is the doctrine that most non-Mormons *think* Latter-day Saints believe and, on the other, there is the doctrine that they actually *do* believe. It is my hope to shed some light on a very misunderstood and "peculiar people" (1 Peter 2:9) by dispelling some of the myths that surround this Church. (Unless otherwise indicated, all biblical scriptures are taken from the King James Version of the Holy Bible). Perhaps it will then become a little more apparent "why anyone would want to belong to the Mormon Church."

It is my hope that this book will demonstrate to the reader that the beliefs and practices of the Latter-day Saints — that is, the Mormons — are in complete harmony with the scriptural record known as the Holy Bible. Non-Mormons will learn firsthand, from someone who has made the transition from mainstream Christianity to LDS Christianity, about a wide range of gospel doctrines as they are embraced by the Latter-day Saints. Members of the Church will likewise benefit, as their testimonies of the restored gospel will be strengthened and their scriptural knowledge will be enhanced by the in-depth treatment of fundamental LDS doctrines from a biblical perspective. Full-time and stake missionaries, new converts, and seminary students will find this book particularly helpful as they endeavor to increase their gospel knowledge, as well as discover the historical and scriptural validity of the restoration of Jesus Christ's gospel and Church.

1

MY PERSONAL QUEST FOR TRUTH

UNDER the cloak of darkness, Nicodemus, a member of the Jewish sect known as the Pharisees, sought the counsel of a man despised by others of his sect — a man whose teachings and actions were at the center of controversy. The man he sought was the same man we should all be sincerely seeking — the Lord Jesus Christ. In response to one of Nicodemus' inquiries, the Lord conveyed an important eternal truth that has implications for each of us: "Verily, verily, I say unto thee, Except a man be born of water and of the Spirit, he cannot enter into the kingdom of God" (John 3:5). A few years later, the resurrected Lord gave the charge to His apostles to "preach the gospel to every creature," then added, "He that believeth and is baptized shall be saved" (Mark 16:15-16).

On February 21, 1981, I took this divine counsel to heart as I entered the waters of baptism, thereby joining The Church of Jesus Christ of Latter-day Saints. Despite my excitement to join the Lord's Church, I was somewhat apprehensive about sharing the news of my baptism with my family, as I was unsure of their reaction. In fact, the day before my baptism, I still had not informed my mother of my decision. Thinking my mother already knew, my half-brother, also a convert to the Church, inadvertently disclosed the news during a telephone conversation while I was still building up courage.

He called her the night before my baptism to find out how she felt about my decision to join the Church. It wasn't very long before he realized that she knew nothing of my investigation into the Church, much less my decision to be baptized. He determined that it was too late to retract what was already said and allow me the opportunity to make the formal invitation, therefore he took it upon himself to invite her. He then called me immediately to share the details of this unexpected conversation, partly to chastise me for procrastinating and partly to warn me in light of her less-than-positive response to the news. I could hardly blame my mother for her shocked and disappointed reaction. After all, everything she had ever heard about the Church was hardly flattering or uplifting, and she was sincerely concerned for the welfare of her son.

Now that she had been invited to attend my baptism, I saw little reason to call her before the actual event. The procrastination and the associated drama would continue, as we would not speak until the time of the baptismal service. I stepped out of the dressing room wearing the customary white baptismal clothing and entered the room where the baptismal service would take place. I'll never forget the look on her face as our eyes met. What in the world would motivate her son, who came from a long line of Lutherans, to join the Mormon Church? This was so out of character for him. This was how I interpreted her concerned expression as I approached to thank her for attending my baptism. I smiled sheepishly at her, and she forced a smile in return. Much went unsaid until I later arrived at her house after the baptism.

About an hour and a half later, we found ourselves sitting uncomfortably in her living room. Not wishing to postpone the inevitable any longer, I finally asked, "So, what did you think of my baptism?" Not a great opening line, but it cleared the way for further discussion.

"I'm very surprised. Why didn't you tell me earlier?"

"Well, it all happened so fast, and I wasn't sure how you would react."

There was further silence. I could detect a deep-seated concern in her eyes. I decided to delve deeper, "You seem to be disappointed by my decision to be baptized. Why?"

Her response came without any hesitation. I then learned why she accepted the news of my baptism with so much anxiety and consternation. "You don't even believe in Jesus Christ."

I suddenly realized that I had much to overcome in the way of misinformation. It would take time and patience to overcome years of accumulated misconceptions regarding the Church. I replied to her heartfelt concern, "Did you know that the real name of the Church is The Church of Jesus Christ of Latter-day Saints, not the Mormon Church? That would be a strange name to give the Church if we didn't believe in Jesus Christ. We believe He is the Son of God and the Savior of the world. That's one of the reasons I joined His Church."

This brief conversation about LDS beliefs was the first of many that my mother and I have had regarding church doctrine. For the past 17 years, I have continued to share various beliefs and practices of the Church with my mother, as the occasion arises. Since then, she has become very supportive of my decision to join the Lord's Church, as she has witnessed the benefits and blessings it has reaped for me and my immediate family. I believe that my decision to be baptized into the Lord's Church has brought my mother and me closer together, as we more greatly appreciate our similarities as well as respect our differences.

My baptism signified both an ending and a beginning in my life. It represented the culmination of a five-year quest for eternal truth and the purpose of life, as well as the beginning of a new life of spiritual growth and development. Although I always believed myself to be a happy, well-balanced individual, there were certain unanswered questions that weighed heavily upon my mind that prevented me from achieving total happiness and personal fulfillment.

Throughout my life, I felt that there had to be a higher purpose to my existence, and in particular, to my placement on this earth. I knew that I could never be truly happy until I learned where I came from, why I was here, and where I was going after death. I wanted to see the big picture and where I fit in that picture. I grew tired of the lifestyle wherein we "eat, drink, and be merry," never giving much thought to life's profounder issues.

In discussing the purpose of life, a popular LDS scholar effectively employs an insightful analogy. He likens the world to a schoolground wherein the assigned students get sidetracked by the playground equipment. They are so busy playing with the swings and teeter-totters that they are oblivious to the school buildings located across the playground. Fully preoccupied by their entertainment and content to remain on the playground, they never wander over to the classrooms to discover the great learning taking place or the higher purpose for which the school was built. So it goes for the world at large. Most of God's children appear to be so distracted by food, clothes, sports, careers, popularity, entertainment, wealth, power, pleasure, and the like, that they never look beyond these superficial pursuits in order to discover God's higher purpose for us on earth.

I finally reached a point in my life when I wanted to get off the proverbial swings, wander over to the classrooms, and take a peek in the door to see what was to be learned about the meaning of life. Although I was raised in a Protestant home, I found it difficult to remain truly devoted to the religion of my ancestors. While it contained much truth and many good, God-fearing people, I felt it truly lacked something. Some of the pieces of the puzzle to the purpose of life were still missing. I slowly drifted to the ranks of the agnostics, those who are not committed to total belief or disbelief but are continuing the search for answers to their persistent questions about life. I was not comfortable in my disbelief, yet I found it even more difficult to believe in God based on the doctrines which were presented to me during my youth as gospel truths.

As the desire grew within me to find the answers to my deepest questions, I was motivated to embark on a five-year quest for the purpose of my personal existence. I don't mean to imply that I dropped out of life to spend my days in the seclusion of a Tibetan monastery — quite the contrary. I continued to work and attend college, as well as socialize with my regular circle of friends, who were undoubtedly oblivious to my growing hunger for universal truth. However, every chance I could find, I would read books, attend seminars, or simply investigate other religions and philosophies — Christian and non-Christian alike. Many of these belief systems seemed to possess elements of truth, however, nothing struck me as the body of thought that could answer all of my questions satisfactorily or show me the big picture.

Although I pressed on with my search, I began to think that the knowledge I was seeking was unattainable or too elusive. Then I came across a book on near-death experiences which was instrumental in moving me away from atheism and agnosticism toward a belief in spiritual things. Shortly thereafter, a friend loaned me a book on current events as they related to biblical prophecy. This was helpful in redirecting my search back toward Christianity. For a period, I had abandoned Christianity as a possibility, since I thought all Christian churches harbored the same mainstream Christian beliefs that I was taught as a youth. A closer look at Christendom revealed an incredible diversity of doctrines — a fact which piqued my interest in Christian theology once again.

One evening, in an act of desperation, I went to a nearby reservoir, drove onto the the public access area of the dam, parked my car, and not knowing who or what, if anything, was out there to hear me, began to pour my heart out to the vast heavens stretching infinitely before me. As I gazed skyward, overwhelmed by the beauty and majesty of the Milky Way, I contemplated my own relative insignificance, then offered the closest thing to a prayer that an agnostic could muster. My appeals to know the purpose of life were heartfelt and sincere, yet my predicament still seemed hopeless and inescapable.

This was the last resort for someone who felt he had searched the world over for eternal truth. I thought if there really was a God, then he must know the truth, and surely he must have a desire to share that truth with me. It made logical sense to approach this being with my dilemma, therefore, from the depths of my soul I pleaded my case to him that evening, all the while my eyes focused on the stars above. After spending an indeterminable amount of time conversing with the heavens, I left the dam that evening wondering if I was heard, and, if I was, how and when would I receive an answer?

I didn't have to wait very long. As I continued to ponder my quest for truth, it dawned on me that my older half-brother had recently joined a church. Knowing that he had at one time exhibited similar agnostic tendencies to those I currently possessed, I was determined to learn why he joined a church and found a renewed faith in God. Over the course of the next few months, we had several discussions that took us into the late hours of the evening.

As we discussed the meaning of man's existence and other weighty matters, I was authentically surprised by the things my brother had to say. Not only was I intrigued by his church's beliefs, but for the first time in my search I found something that immediately impressed me as being true. It seemed as if I had known and espoused these beliefs my entire life, but I needed to hear someone else express them in order to revive them from their dormant state. Nearly all the questions I had about my existence, the purpose of life, and the plan of salvation were answered in a simple, coherent manner. I knew that I had to learn more about this church and its doctrine. The church that taught such clear doctrine turned out to be The Church of Jesus Christ of Latter-day Saints, also known as the Mormon Church.

After several late night gospel discussions, my brother introduced me to a couple of young men serving two-year missions for the Church. One Sunday afternoon, as the missionaries arrived at my brother's home, I waited for them in the living room, sitting on a couch with my back to the front door where they entered. Upon seeing my long hair, they immediately thought that they must have misunderstood my brother, for they thought he told them that his brother — not his sister — was interested in hearing about the gospel! As I stood up and turned to greet them, they quickly realized that they had not misunderstood. Perhaps the moustache was a giveaway.

I was very impressed by these young men, especially their friendly demeanor and enthusiasm for life. After lunch and small talk, we engaged in a more serious discussion in which they taught me many things that I had never before heard regarding the restoration of the fullness of the gospel of Jesus Christ to the earth. To this day, the thing that I remember most about our discussion is the way that I felt about the principles and concepts I was taught.

Before we started our discussion, the missionaries asked if we could open our informal meeting with a prayer. I told the missionaries to proceed and one of them offered an unpretentious and sincere prayer to our Heavenly Father in the name of Jesus Christ. As we opened our eyes following the prayer, the missionaries looked at me with a smile and asked how I felt. I told them that I felt good, but I also felt an inner warmth that I couldn't describe. The best way that I could explain it at the time was to say that I felt like I had heartburn without the pain — it was a comforting, reassuring feeling residing in the bosom. They explained that they also felt it, and that I was feeling the influence of the Holy Ghost. The Holy Ghost's role is to testify of the Father and the Son, and his presence there, that day, was to testify to me that the things the missionaries shared with me relative to Jesus Christ and his gospel were true. I felt that divine influence throughout the remainder of our discussion.

I was fascinated by the things I heard that day, but remained unsure as to their truthfulness. The missionaries challenged me to ponder and pray about the things we discussed. They also gave me a copy of the Book of Mormon, a book that they claimed was a companion book of scripture to the Holy Bible. They asked me if I would read the pages they marked, then ask God if what I read was true. I was impressed that they didn't expect me to believe them or take their word for it, but instead encouraged me to go directly to God with my questions. I told them that I wasn't even sure if there was a God, however, I really did have a sincere desire to know if their teachings were true. I also could see the profound implications of the things they had taught me, therefore I told them that I would accept their challenge to read, ponder, and pray.

That night before I retired for the evening, I knelt at the foot of my bed to pray for divine guidance. It was probably the first formal, sincere prayer of my life. I began my humble appeal, "Dear God, if there even is a God, please help me to find the truth..." A few minutes later, I arose from my kneeling prayer not feeling any different, but knowing that I had done my best to approach the throne of almighty God.

The next day I found some time alone to read the Book of Mormon. At first, I found it very interesting but not particularly earth-shattering. After finishing the 20 pages or so that the missionaries had marked, I decided to turn back to the first page of the book and continue reading. I became enthralled as I read about a Hebrew prophet from Jerusalem who took his family to the land of the Americas in a boat his sons built by inspiration from God. I was fascinated by the visions he had and prophecies he made, especially as they related to the promised land — the land of America.

As I continued to read chapter after chapter, I lost all concept of time and my surroundings. I became so engrossed in what I was reading that before I knew it, I had read the first 15 chapters of the book. Eventually, I began to sense that something was happening to me — something that I had never before experienced, something quite wonderful. I felt as if I was filled simultaneously with light and joy from head to toe. Placing the book on my lap, my only desire was to bask in the warmth of this unseen light.

As I sat on the couch, enjoying and contemplating this marvelous experience, I had the irresistible urge to laugh and cry at the same time — and so I did. These were not tears of sorrow, but tears of joy. At that moment, I knew that what I had read was true beyond a shadow of a doubt. By the enlightening power of his Spirit — the Holy Ghost — my Heavenly Father was communicating to my spirit that the Book of Mormon was the word of God. As I arrived at the realization that this sacred volume was scripture, I also realized that Joseph Smith was a prophet of God and The Church of Jesus Christ of Latter-day Saints was Christ's restored Church. As pure intelligence seemed to pour into me through the Lord's Spirit, the principle of truth that had the greatest impact on me was this: for the first time in my life, I knew as sure as the sun was shining that I was a child of a living God who loves me with an infinite love, and that he does answer sincere prayer. I knew then, as I know now, that God has a plan for each one of us to gain eternal life — an eternal life of happiness in his glorious kingdom.

I also learned something about the true purpose of life. I learned that we are not placed here on earth to satisfy our vain desires but to do God's will. He has sent us here to this proving ground known as mortality to gain a physical body and see if we will obey his commandments as we walk in faith. If we exercise faith in Christ, repent of our sins, and prove ourselves worthy of his grace, we will receive an eternal life of joy. The experiences we have during this mortal probation will prepare us for a greater glory in heaven, as we endeavor to fulfill our divine destiny as sons and daughters of God.

I knew these things were true, for I received them from the source of all light and truth — my Heavenly Father. I had truly communed with God. I no longer relied on any other person for truth, for God had taught me directly from on high. With these eternal truths indelibly stamped on my heart and mind, nothing could keep me from the waters of baptism. I desired to demonstrate my faith in Christ by following his admonition to be baptized in His Church. Which brings us back full circle to the beginning of this book and the question posed by its title, "Why would anyone join the Mormon Church?"

The only person who could have ever wrought such a mighty change in my heart and convinced me to make such a dramatic change in my life, and to subsequently join this Church, is almighty God Himself. If I hadn't approached God in humility and sincerity, I am sure He never would have responded to my questions the way He did. All my life, my pride kept me off my knees. All my life, I didn't think that I needed anyone else for answers. It wasn't until I finally met God's requirements of humility, sincerity, and diligence that He found me worthy of the knowledge I sought. In order to acquire answers to life's greatest questions, we must admit that we are ignorant before God as we seek the path to eternal life.

Up to this point, I have shared some of the deepest thoughts and feelings I had during my search for the meaning of life and my investigation of the LDS Church. I have said very little regarding the fundamental doctrines of the Church which touched me profoundly as I studied, pondered, and prayed to determine the course God would have me take. Throughout the remainder of this book, I will attempt to convey the gospel truths the Lord has revealed to me by way of His Spirit, His chosen servants, and the scriptures.

The Proper Name of the Church

Before delving into any doctrinal issues, I would like first to address the matter of the proper name of the Church. Although it is commonly referred to as the "Mormon Church," this is simply a nickname initially applied to the Church by nonmembers due to the Church's belief in a book of scripture known as the Book of Mormon. The only true and correct name of the Church is "The Church of Jesus Christ of Latter-day Saints." Since Latter-day Saints equally embrace the inspired writings of the Old and New Testaments of the Holy Bible, it wouldn't make any more sense to call them "Mormons" than it would to call them "Ezekiels," "Isaiahs," "Matthews," "Lukes," or "Peters." And their doctrine is no more "Mormonism" than it is "Jeremiahism," "Danielism," "Johnism," "Jamesism," or "Paulism."[1]

Inasmuch as the proper name of the Church is frequently the source of confusion, an explanation is in order. First, the Church is named after He who stands at its head, that is, Jesus Christ. It is not Paul's church. It is not Peter's church. It is not Luther's church, nor is it anyone else's church. It is the Church of Jesus Christ.

Second, the term "latter-day" is used to differentiate between the Church established during the time of Christ (former days) and the restored Church established today (latter days). The early Church might well be referred to now as The Church of Jesus Christ of Former-day Saints.

Third, the term "saints" simply refers to the church members themselves. This usage of "saint" does not carry the same connotation as that which has developed within other churches. Rather than implying canonization, perfection, or an exalted status, it is used in the same way that the Apostle Paul applied it during the time of the early Christian Church when he wrote to "the *saints* which are at Ephesus" (Ephesians 1:1), "the church of God which is at Corinth, to them that are sanctified in Christ Jesus, *called to be saints*" (1 Corinthians 1:1), or any of the other branches of the Church. (See also Romans 1:7; 1 Corinthians 14:33; 2 Corinthians 1:1; Philippians 1:1; Colossians 1:2; and Hebrews 13:24). Far from being perfect, the saints are simply those who have covenanted to follow the Lord Jesus Christ, thus becoming members of His Church.

That the followers of Christ would be called "saints" in the last days is evidenced by John the Revelator's frequent use of the term when describing the final events leading to Christ's Second Coming. John foretells how the "beast" receives power from Satan "to make war with the saints" in the last days (Revelation 13:7). John later refers to Jesus Christ as the "King of saints" (Revelation 15:3).

John continues with references to the persecutions that the wicked nations of the earth have inflicted upon Christ's disciples and the subsequent judgments awaiting the unrighteous, "for they have shed the blood of saints and prophets" (Revelation 16:6; 17:6; 18:24). Finally, he reveals how Satan and his evil forces will have "compassed the camp of the saints about" only to be destroyed by the power of the Almighty God of heaven and earth (Revelation 20:9). The scriptures clearly demonstrate that the followers of Jesus Christ, in the past as well as today, are referred to as "saints."

LATTER-DAY SAINTS ARE CHRISTIANS

I have frequently heard misinformed individuals say that Latter-day Saints are not true Christians. Some even believe that Latter-day Saints worship Joseph Smith or Mormon or some other person. Nothing could be further from the truth. Members of the LDS Church worship God, the Eternal Father, in the name of His Son, Jesus Christ. When Latter-day Saints pray, they pray to the

Father in the name of the Son. They believe the ultimate form of worship consists of emulating the Savior Himself by wholeheartedly accepting His gospel, abiding by His gospel principles in daily life, and observing all His holy commandments.

As Latter-day Saints, we believe that Jesus Christ is the Son of God, the Only Begotten of the Father, and that by Him the heavens and earth were created. We believe that He is the Savior of all mankind, and that there is no other name under heaven whereby man may be saved. We believe that He sweat great drops of blood from every pore as He bore the sins of the world while in the Garden of Gethsemane, and that He culminated his great atoning sacrifice upon the cross at Calvary where Roman soldiers drove nails through His hands, wrists, and feet.

We believe that Christ died upon the cross, and on the third day He rose from the dead in his glorious resurrection to sit upon the right hand of God. We believe that He will return to earth at some future time, coming in power and glory with legions of angels, to reign as God and King, and to stand as Judge of all mankind. This is the Jesus Christ that we revere, honor, and obey.

LATTER-DAY SAINT BELIEF IN THE BIBLE

It is also a popular misconception that Latter-day Saints do not believe in the inspired writings of the Holy Bible. It is alleged, again incorrectly, that LDS doctrine is not in harmony with biblical scripture. The fact of the matter is that Latter-day Saints do not always subscribe to the commonly accepted, present-day interpretations of certain biblical passages, which occasionally leads others to the conclusion that Latter-day Saints do not accept the Bible.

It would be more accurate to say that while we do accept the Bible as scripture, we do not accept certain beliefs or post-New Testament creeds which are so popular today. Rather, we profess to share beliefs and practices with the early Christians of the first century. Throughout this book, I will attempt to demonstrate that LDS beliefs are supported by, although not exclusively reliant upon, biblical scripture and the teachings of the early Christians.

LATTER-DAY SAINT PRACTICES

In addition to the doctrinal teachings of the Latter-day Saints, their wholesome lifestyle was also instrumental in my spiritual conversion to the LDS faith. Granting some exceptions, practicing Latter-day Saints are some of the most charitable, honest, trustworthy, clean, righteous, chaste, loyal, and God-fearing people I have ever known. However far from perfect, they are nevertheless zealous in their observance of God's commandments (Titus 2:14).

Practicing Latter-day Saints do not smoke, drink alcohol, abuse drugs, or profane. Married Latter-day Saints practice fidelity in their marriages while single members exercise chastity in their relationships. They endeavor to be honest in all dealings with their fellow man, be they private or public.

They are patriotic citizens willing to defend their country as well as God-given freedoms throughout the world. History testifies that they have served their country even when their own rights have been denied. They believe in obeying the laws of the land (Matthew 22:21; Titus 3:1; 1 Peter 2:13). They love and support the Constitution of the United States and recognize it as a divinely-inspired document designed to preserve the God-given rights to life, liberty, and property of every American.

They voluntarily donate much of their hard-earned money for the feeding and clothing of the poor. They pray for the welfare of others and offer assistance to the sick and afflicted. They donate hours of their time to church and community service. As their Thirteenth Article of Faith states, "We believe in being honest, true, chaste, benevolent, virtuous, and in doing good to all men...If there is anything virtuous, lovely, or of good report or praiseworthy, we seek after these things." In short, they believe in loving and serving God and their fellow man with all their heart, might, mind, and strength.

I should add that as Latter-day Saints "we claim the privilege of worshiping Almighty God according to the dictates of our own conscience, and allow all men the same privilege, let them worship how, where, or what they may" (Eleventh Article of Faith). That is to say, we respect the rights of others to believe and worship as they please, embracing the constitutional provision of freedom of religion, and find neither pleasure in nor reason to defame, alter, or belittle those religious principles held sacred by other denominations. We even defend the rights of others to worship as they may and would hope that they might extend the same courtesy to us. Religious tolerance is indeed a divine attribute that would become all people, for each one of us, regardless of religious or nonreligious affiliation, is truly a child of God.

2

THE TRUE NATURE OF THE GODHEAD

GROWING up as a mainstream Protestant, I often reflected on the nature of God and my relationship with Him (or it, as some surmise). Who was God? What was He like? What did He look like? Did He really fill the universe? Why did He create me? Why did He put me on this planet called earth? Was He really one being with three aspects or personalities — the Father, Son, and Holy Ghost — or were these three actually separate beings in their own right? Was God really male or did we simply refer to God as "Him" out of tradition?

One reason I pondered these questions regarding the nature of God was to gain a better understanding of who He was, which in turn, would give me a better understanding of who I was as well as my relationship with Him and what He expected of me. Was God a non-material essence that filled all space? If He was, then why did He create me — a puny being with two arms, two legs, and a head — and why did He then say that I was created in His image? Why wouldn't He create beings who were more like Himself? And if I wasn't really like Him, then why does He refer to Himself as our Father, and us as His sons and daughters? As I sought the responses to these questions, I had very little success in finding satisfactory answers.

What joy did God get from creating little creatures who had no similarity to Him in physical appearance, intellectual abilities, or spiritual characteristics? One can only get so much satisfaction from observing an ant farm. And once a portion of His creatures were saved by His good graces and permitted to live in His presence, what would they do for an eternity? Would we ever be able to communicate with God at His level? What exactly was the purpose of our existence?

Finally, why was I taught that the Father — an immaterial being who filled the universe — was the same being as the flesh and blood Son who walked the earth and the same being as the non-physical Holy Ghost who enlightened our minds? I was taught that each was a person but each was not a being, for they together comprised one being in total. Wasn't a person also a being? If the Father was a person, wasn't He also a being? If Jesus Christ was a person, wasn't

He also a being, even a human being? When pursuing such logic, one is told not to try to understand the incomprehensibility of God, for it is truly a mystery.

I was not so easily dissuaded, and I continued my quest for truth. It wasn't until I met members of the LDS Church that I received the answers to my lifelong questions. As you will discover from the following pages in this chapter and others, God really is comprehensible. He is our literal Father and we are his literal children. This simple truth is taught by prophets of our day, just as it was taught by prophets of old.

LDS BELIEFS REGARDING THE GODHEAD

One reason for my association with the LDS Church is the clarity of its teachings regarding the nature and characteristics of the Godhead. As Latter-day Saints, we believe that we have but one God comprised of three separate and distinct personages — God, the Father; his Son, Jesus Christ; and the Holy Ghost. These three alone — this triad of holy beings — constitute the Godhead, or divine governing body of heaven and earth.

We do not subscribe to the belief that these three divine beings are merely different manifestations or aspects of the same divine essence, power, or being. We do not believe that the Father is His own son, and the Son, His own father. As Latter-day Saints, we believe that three distinct persons constitute one God — or Godhead — in purpose, while dismissing the notion that these three are of the same undivided substance or essence.

While the differences might seem trivial, they are indeed critical, since the scriptures teach us that "this is life eternal, that they might know thee the only true God, and Jesus Christ, whom thou hast sent" (John 17:3). Our very salvation depends on our proper worship of the true God. Latter-day Saints do not believe that God is incomprehensible to the human understanding. In fact, the scriptures teach that a true knowledge of God is essential to our salvation. Just as a proper understanding of another individual is crucial to any interpersonal relationship, a sound understanding of God is crucial to our relationship with Him. How can we be expected to have faith, a faith that influences both thought and action, unless we know and understand the very object of that faith?

THE GODHEAD: THREE SEPARATE BEINGS

The scriptures clearly teach that our Heavenly Father, our Savior,

Jesus Christ, and the Holy Ghost, are three separate and distinct individuals. At his baptism, as Jesus came "up out of the water, he saw the heavens opened, and the Spirit, like a dove, descending upon him: and there came a voice from heaven saying, "Thou art my beloved Son, in whom I am well pleased" (Mark 1:10-11). Here is an event at which each member of the Godhead was simultaneously manifested, thus demonstrating their distinctness. As Jesus came out of the water, a voice from heaven declared His divine Sonship while the Holy Ghost descended upon Him from above.

When Stephen, a disciple of Christ, declared, "Behold, I see the heavens opened, and the Son of man standing on the right hand of God" (Acts 7:56), he saw two distinct individuals, one standing on the right hand of the other.

In the Garden of Gethsemane, Christ "fell on his face, and prayed, saying, O my Father…" (Matthew 26:39). Are we to believe that Christ was praying to Himself? Or was He praying to His Father, a being as distinct from the Son as one man is from another?

In that same garden, Christ went on to plead with His Father, "If it be possible, let this cup pass from me; nevertheless *not as I will, but as thou wilt*" (Matthew 26:39). Here is a demonstration of two separate wills or desires in operation. For a time, Christ's will was not the Father's will. On another occasion, the Savior taught the Jews in Jerusalem, "I seek not mine own will, but the will of the Father which hath sent me" (John 5:30). These statements of the Savior could only be true and meaningful if the Father and the Son were indeed two distinct individuals each possessing His own mind and will.

During His mortal ministry, the Savior declared, "For the Father judgeth no man, but hath committed all judgment unto the Son" (John 5:22). The Son, not the Father, is the eternal Judge of all mankind. If the Father and Son are the same being or of the same substance, how can one be something the other is not?

Speaking of his Second Coming, the Savior said, "But of that day and that hour knoweth no man, no, not the angels which are in heaven, *neither the Son, but the Father*" (Mark 13:32; Matthew 24:36). The Father was the only one who knew the time of Christ's return, demonstrating that the Father possessed knowledge that the Son did not. Again, this characterizes their distinct and separate nature and identities.

During the creation, God said, "Let us make man in *our* image, after *our* likeness" (Genesis 1:26). Later, after Adam and Eve had eaten the forbidden fruit, God said, "Behold, the man is become as one of *us*" (Genesis 3:22). This language clearly indicates a plurality of individuals, one speaking to the other. The Savior taught, "And whosoever speaketh a word against the Son of man [Jesus Christ], it shall be forgiven him: but whosoever speaketh against the Holy Ghost, it shall *not* be forgiven him" (Matthew 12:32). This distinction would be superfluous save the Savior and the Holy Ghost were two separate and distinct beings.

In one of his letters to Timothy, Paul wrote that "there is one God, and one mediator between God and men, the man Christ Jesus" (1 Timothy 2:5). In other words, the Son is the mediator or advocate who stands between us and our Heavenly Father, indicating at least three separate parties. In both Greek and English, the word "mediator" is a legal term indicating a "middleman" or "third person" standing between two estranged parties who attempts to bring them together.[1] The Savior is our advocate, our mediator, or if you please, our defense attorney, pleading our case to the Father in our behalf in the celestial courts on high. Once again, the terminology used and relationships represented clearly indicate the distinct nature of the Father and his Son.

On one occasion, a young man approached the Savior while inquiring, "Good Master, what good thing shall I do, that I may have eternal life?" Jesus responded, "Why callest thou me good? There is none good but one, that is, God" (Matthew 19:16-17). The Savior emphasized his distinctiveness from the Father by indicating that the Father was truly good and perfect in a sense that the Son was not. The Savior drew a clear distinction between Himself and His Father; the Father was better than the Son, something hardly possible if they were of the same undivided substance. This is consistent with the Savior's statement, "My Father is greater than I" (John 14:28). How can one be greater than the other if they are the same being or of one undivided substance?

During one of his discourses, the Savior was accused by the Pharisees of lacking sufficient testimonial support for His claims of Messiahship. "The Pharisees therefore said unto him, Thou bearest record of thyself; thy record is not true" (John 8:13). Part of the Savior's response is very revealing: "And yet if I judge, my judgment is true: for *I am not alone*, but I and the Father that sent me. It is also written in your law, that *the testimony of two men is true. I am one that bear witness of myself, and the Father that sent me beareth witness of me*" (John 8:16-18). Having been accused of bearing witness of himself, the Savior declared He had the testimonies of two individuals, Himself and His Father, thereby fulfilling the requirements of the law.

No one knows the Father as well as His Beloved Son, and it was the Savior Himself that frequently taught that He came not to do His own will, but the will of the Father. This would have been an unnecessary distinction if the Father and the Son were one being or of one substance. Consider the Savior's response to an inquiry made regarding his teachings: *"My doctrine is not mine, but his that sent me. If any man will do his will, he shall know of the doctrine, whether it be of God [the Father], or whether I speak of myself [God, the Son]. He that speaketh of himself seeketh his own glory:* but he that seeketh his glory that sent him, the same is true, and no unrighteousness is in him" (John 7:16-18).

This statement of the Savior's is rich in knowledge regarding the nature of the Godhead. It establishes the following points: 1) the Father sent the Son; 2) the doctrine that Christ taught was not His own, but the Father's; and 3) Christ did not speak of Himself, but of the Father. Any effort to interpret these clear and beautiful teachings so as to promote the idea that the Father and the Son are one and the same being or substance would only distort the true intended message.

GOD'S ETERNAL FAMILY

Hopefully, these scriptures will have sufficiently demonstrated the true nature of the Godhead; the Father, Son, and Holy Ghost are three separate individuals. The Savior even taught us concerning our own relationship with the Father and himself when He said to Mary Magdalene after his resurrection, "Touch me not: for I am not yet ascended to *my Father:* but go to my brethren, and say unto them, I ascend unto *my Father,* and *your Father;* and to *my God,* and *your God"* (John 20:17).

The same familial relationship that exists between our Heavenly Father and Christ also exists between the Father and us. The Savior's Father is also our Father, and yet we are not one in substance or being with Him. He is the Father of our spirits and we are His offspring (Hebrews 12:9; Acts 17:29). We are physically separate and distinct from Him, as is the Savior. Jesus Christ, the firstborn among the Father's spirit children (Romans 8:29; Hebrews 1:6), is our elder brother, making us all part of the same great eternal family.

While speaking to Mary Magdalene after His resurrection, Christ referred to the Father as His God (John 20:17). The Father is the God of the Son. This demonstrates a hierarchy of beings. Our Heavenly Father and our Savior cannot be the same being, since the Father is the God of Jesus Christ, His Son.

THE ONENESS OF GOD

If the scriptures are so clear in revealing the distinct nature of the three members of the Godhead, then why do some people believe that the Father, Son, and Holy Ghost are one and the same being or essence? The answer lies partially in their interpretation of certain biblical passages. The Savior declared to the Jews, "I and my Father are one" (John 10:30). Was Christ trying to teach the Jews that He and His Father were one and the same being, or did He have another intended meaning of oneness in mind? In His first epistle, the Apostle John wrote, "For there are three that bear record in heaven, the Father, the Word, and the Holy Ghost: and these three are one" (1 John 5:7). Did John mean that the three members of the Godhead are one being? Again, the answer is found in the scriptures.

During His great intercessory prayer, Christ prayed to the Father in His disciples' behalf, pleading, "Neither pray I for these alone, but for them also which shall believe on me through their word; that they all may be *one*; as thou, Father, art in me, and I in thee, that they also may be *one* in us: that the world may believe that thou hast sent me. And the glory which thou gavest me I have given them; that *they may be one, even as we are one*" (John 17:20-22).

We may become "one" with the Father even as Christ is "one" with Him. If we are to interpret the oneness of the Father and the Son as a reference to their physical identity or their oneness of essence, then we must ascribe this same oneness of being to all of Christ's disciples. Are we to believe that all Christians will fuse into one great essence with the Father and Christ? That would be unthinkable. The oneness of God refers to the unity of love, purpose, spirit, mind, power, and righteousness that exists between the Father, Son, and Holy Ghost.

Concerning Christ's statement, "I and my Father are one" (John 10:30), in the original Greek texts the word "one" appears in the neuter gender which indicates oneness in attributes, power, or purpose. For it to imply a oneness of being, personality, or identity, the masculine form of the word would be required.[2]

The Savior used similar language when commenting on the unity shared by husband and wife: "For this cause shall a man leave his father and mother, and cleave to his wife; and *they twain shall be one flesh*: so then they are no more twain, but one flesh" (Mark 10:7-8). As in the earlier quoted scriptures regarding the oneness of the Godhead, it is obvious that the Lord is alluding to a unity of mind and purpose, and not physical fusion.

Speaking to an errant Israel, the Lord proclaimed, "Ye are my witnesses, saith the Lord, and my servant whom I have chosen: that ye may know and believe me, and understand that I am he: *before me there was no God formed*, neither shall there be after me" (Isaiah 43:10). This scripture must be understood in the proper cultural context. First, after settling the promised land, the Israelites began to assume the idolatrous practices of their new pagan neighbors. They worshiped a multitude of graven images of stone and wood, creating manmade gods that governed various aspects of their lives and the world around them. A greater spiritual blindness is difficult to imagine. This explains the Lord's simplistic teaching to His spiritually immature children. They were not spiritually prepared to receive or understand the full doctrine of the Godhead.

Second, strictly speaking, the idolatrous Israelites had only one God, namely, Jehovah. It was the pre-mortal Son of God, Jehovah, that directed the Israelites through the wilderness to the promised land, and it was He that spoke for and in behalf of the Father. (A comparison of a few biblical scriptures will illustrate that Jesus Christ of the New Testament was also Jehovah of the Old Testament: Isaiah 43:3,11 and Luke 2:11; Exodus 3:14 and John 8:54-58; Deuteronomy 32:2-4 and 1 Corinthians 10:1-4).

Christ also admonished, "Believe me that I am in the Father, and the Father in me" (John 14:11). Does this mean that the Father and the Son are the same being or of the same substance? Further reading will reveal the answer: "At that day ye shall know that I am in my Father, and *ye [disciples] in me, and I in you*" (John 14:20). The Savior is obviously referring to the Spirit of God or harmony of love and purpose that exists between the Father, Son, and true disciples.

Latter-day Saints believe that each member of the Godhead enjoys the status of personhood and Godhood and that each is a being in his own right, separate and unique from the others who comprise the Godhead. The Godhead consists of three beings, three persons, or three Gods who are one in purpose. We believe the scriptures clearly testify of this fact.

Origen, a Church scholar living from A.D. 185-253, was quite familiar with the early Christian doctrine of the Godhead. He taught that the Son is "other in subsistence [existence] than the Father" and that the Father and the Son "are two things in respect of Their Persons, but one in unanimity, harmony and identity of will...We are not afraid to speak in one sense of *two Gods*, in another sense of one God."[3] In other words, the Father and Son are two Gods in the sense of their distinct identities, but are one God in the sense of their goals, desires, and purposes for the eternal salvation of mankind.

It is interesting to note that the term "trinity" is not once used by the Lord's prophets or apostles. Nowhere within the pages of the Holy Bible can terminology such as "trinity," "triad," "triune," or anything like it be found. The term "trinity," or the Latin term "trinitas," was first used by Tertullian, a lawyer by trade and

Christian by faith, who lived from A.D. 160-220. The term first appeared in his work, Against Praxeas, around A.D. 210, therefore the terminology of the Trinity did not even begin its development until over 110 years after the disappearance of the last apostle.[4]

The fully developed doctrine of the Trinity traces its roots to the man-made creeds of a changing, post-apostolic Christendom, formalized during a period of unprecedented spiritual darkness. According to J.N.D. Kelly of Oxford, England, a renowned scholar of early Christian writings, "Not until the council of Constantinople (381) was the formula of one God existing in three co-equal Persons formally ratified."[5]

Even so, the trinitarian doctrine of God was not completely defined until the early fifth century when Augustine of Hippo had appeared on the scene. "It was Augustine, however, who gave the Western tradition [of the Trinity] its mature and final expression."[6] Augustine combined elements of scripture and philosophy to formulate the popular definition of the Godhead, thereby consummating and formalizing five centuries of debate and speculation.

THE APOSTASY AND THE DOCTRINE OF THE GODHEAD

There are other historical and philosophical factors contributing to the widespread, present-day acceptance of the trinitarian concept of the Godhead as propounded in the councils of Nicaea (A.D. 325), Constantinople (381), Ephesus (431), and Chalcedon (451). The early Christians were accused of blasphemy by the Jews due to their belief in the divinity of Jesus Christ. The Jews reasoned that if the Father was God, and the Son was also God, this implied a plurality of Gods, which they believed threatened their strict monotheistic views. After all, didn't the ancient scriptures say, "Hear, O Israel: The Lord our God is one Lord" (Deuteronomy 6:4)? They dismissed the idea that this oneness of God, this principle of monotheism, could refer to the Godhead's unity of purpose and not unity of substance.

The record shows that the early Christians believed in a Godhead comprised of three distinct beings, as a study of early Christian writings will attest, giving rise to accusations of polytheism by Jewish authorities. Early Church "Fathers" living prior to the Council of Nicaea such as Clement, Ignatius, Hermas, Justin Martyr, and Origen, believed that the Father, Son, and Holy Ghost were three numerically distinct persons.[7] This embarrassed many early Christians who regarded the plain and simple doctrine of the Godhead as naive and unsophisticated.

As a result, influential parties within the early Christian Church felt compelled to meld the three members of the Godhead into one single being or substance by some linguistic legerdemain or semantic sophistry in order to preserve the dignity of their persecuted religion. They set themselves to the task of utilizing the philosophies of men in an attempt to argue that God (or the Godhead) was a one-in-three, three-in-one being.

J.N.D. Kelly of Oxford wrote that "it was out of the raw material thus provided by the preaching, worshipping Church that theologians had to construct their more sophisticated accounts of the Christian doctrine of the Godhead."[8] In other words, after the death of the living apostles and prophets, uninspired zealots equipped with the philosophies of men wasted no time in changing the pure teachings of Jesus Christ in order to establish a church after their own liking.

In an ancient document entitled "The Epistle of Peter to Jacob 2," the Apostle Peter is credited with anticipating the matter of doctrinal distortion: "They think they are able to interpret my own words better than I can, telling their hearers that they are conveying my very thoughts to them, while the fact is that such things never entered my mind. If they take such outrageous liberties while I am alive, what will they do after I am gone?"[9] The ensuing creeds of the theologians and philosophers which replaced the simple teachings of the apostles leave us little to wonder about what they did after Peter and the other apostles were gone.

A development that contributed to this embellishment of the doctrine of the Godhead was the coercive involvement of the Roman Emperor, Constantine, a sun worshipper who murdered his own wife and son for the love of worldly power and gain. Constantine, who assumed control of the Christian Church as a means to solidify his own political rule, entered the scene when this internal Church dispute concerning the nature of the Godhead had been raging for some time. He therefore called for a council of the Church to be held in the city of Nicaea in A.D. 325, over which he would preside in order to settle this doctrinal rift.

After hearing arguments presented by the opposing factions, it was Constantine himself that proposed the use of the terminology, "of one essence," to describe the relationship shared by the three members of the Godhead, thus momentarily putting an end to what he considered a trivial issue.[10] At Constantine's request, an official ecclesiastical decree was drawn up, known as the Creed of Nicaea, and those who opposed it were branded heretics or banished. The conflict was forcibly settled and the opposition was temporarily silenced.

In a strong letter to both, Constantine charged the contending camps, "You wrangle with one another over minor, nay, utterly trivial matters."[11] It is incredible that the same man who considered the matter of the true nature of God a trivial matter helped to define that very nature for the entire orthodox Christian community, a definition that has basically remained intact over the centuries and continues to enjoy allegiance even today.

The true doctrine of the Godhead was to remain hidden from the world for many centuries that followed, as this and subsequent councils gave birth to many man-made religious creeds. The authors and proponents of this concept of the Godhead failed to realize that the scriptures testified of the oneness of the Father, Son, and Holy Ghost in terms of their love, purpose, and spiritual harmony and not their physical (or metaphysical) identity.

The highly respected Protestant Bible commentator, J.R. Dummelow, has written that "the exact theological definition of the doctrine of the Trinity was the result of a long process of development, which was not complete until the fifth century, or maybe even later..."[12] The doctrine that the Father, Son, and the Holy Ghost are one and the same being was not taught by the Savior nor his apostles. The historical record clearly shows that it is the gradual product of centuries of debate, confusion, and doctrinal improvisation in a world that had long lost the illuminating spirit of revelation.

The true nature of God is not determined by debate or popular vote in the councils of uninspired men such as took place in Nicaea, but through the channel of divine revelation as received by holy prophets of God. Throughout the ages God has revealed Himself to certain men who have testified to the world, at the peril of their lives, the divine truths which they have been specifically chosen to boldly declare.

Our present age is no exception, as the testimony of the Prophet Joseph Smith demonstrates: "I saw a pillar of light exactly over my head, above the brightness of the sun, which descended gradually until it fell upon me...When the light rested upon me I saw *two Personages*, whose brightness and glory defy all description, standing above me in the air. One of them spake unto me, calling me by name and said, pointing to the other — This is My Beloved Son. Hear Him!"[13] Joseph Smith testified to the world that he saw Jesus Christ standing on the right hand of God, just as Stephen had done centuries before (Acts 7:56), and like Stephen, he died a martyr's death, killed for the boldness and truthfulness of his testimony at the hands of wicked men who could not bear to hear it.

3

THE TRUE NATURE OF GOD THE FATHER

ABOUT a year and a half after I was baptized into the LDS Church, I had a great desire to serve my Heavenly Father by volunteering for a full-time proselyting mission for the Church. I was excited to learn the gospel of Jesus Christ in its fullness, and now I wanted to tell the world about it. Putting both school and career on hold, I submitted the appropriate paperwork to Church headquarters, and before long, I had my mission call to the France Paris Mission. After spending eight weeks in the Missionary Training Center in Provo, Utah, learning about gospel principles and the French language, I was on a 747 headed for the City of Lights — Paris, France.

The day after arriving at the mission home in the suburbs of Paris, I took a nine-hour train ride to a small city in the Basque region of southern France called Biarritz. It was a beautiful coastal city at the foot of the Pyrenees Mountains, situated where the French, Spanish, and Basque cultures converged. My second evening in Biarritz was Christmas Eve, therefore my missionary companion and I (we always worked in pairs) decided to do something very French and very memorable. We went to a Catholic Christmas Eve mass. During the previous few months, my missionary companion and his former companion had occasionally attended choir practices with the local Catholic choir, therefore we both had a desire to see his newfound friends perform before a large congregation.

We rode our bikes several miles in cold weather to arrive just in time for the Christmas mass. The old cathedral was unimpressive from the outside, compared to the likes of Notre Dame in Paris or the great cathedral at Chartres, however from the inside, to me, it was a magnificent structure. And it was full of worshippers. We were satisfied to walk in unnoticed and sit toward the back in order to enjoy this wonderful experience. However, no sooner had we taken our seats, when a kind-looking elderly gentleman approached us and motioned for us to follow him toward the front of the cathedral. My earlier feeling of excitement quickly turned to mild fear.

I would soon learn just how far toward the front he wanted us to sit. He was the choir director, and he was inviting us to join the choir which was situated front and near center — where everyone in the cathedral could get a good look at us. There I was, only my second complete day in France, and I was being asked to sing in a French Catholic choir in a Christmas Eve mass before hundreds, maybe thousands, of people I had never met, and to sing hymns that I had never heard. I am certain that was the Lord's way of making sure that we met as many people as possible, for two Mormon missionaries with dark suits and name plaques standing in the middle of a little French choir were hardly unnoticeable.

Standing amid a small choir of 30 vocalists before a full congregation of parishioners was my first shock for the night. My second shock occurred when the choir director handed the choir booklet to me, containing the hymns and songs for the evening. Not only were we going to sing in French, which I could now manage after eight weeks in the Missionary Training Center in Utah, but we would also sing several numbers in Latin and Basque. Needless to say, I moved my lips a lot without too much sound to accompany my movements. I was glad to be surrounded by hearty, robust voices which carried me through to the end while I did little damage to the wonderful music and worship services.

When the Christmas mass ended, the entire choir, as well as many from the congregation, thanked and congratulated my missionary companion and me for our fine vocal contributions to their choir. We accepted the adulation graciously with smiles and handshakes, not having the heart to confess that the Basque songs proved to be beyond our abilities. As a result of our unplanned musical debut, we made many good friends in this small community of amiable French people. Doors were opened wherever we went in Biarritz as people recognized us from our participation in the choir that evening. I grew to love the French people for their warmth and hospitality.

That night in Biarritz was the first of many visits I made to French cathedrals throughout my mission. I admired the beautiful architecture, sculpture, and artwork in these massive buildings dedicated to the worship of God. It never ceased to amaze me how the artists, whose paintings and murals graced many of those old buildings, depicted the Godhead. Many had similar renditions, but one cathedral in particular — Sacre Coeur in Paris — comes to mind. Above the beautiful altar, on the rounded ceiling, is a marvelous painting of our Heavenly Father with His Son, Jesus Christ, and the Holy Ghost, as represented by a dove. As I gazed up in admiration of this great work of art, I thought how wonderful it was for the true doctrine of the Godhead to be displayed for all who enter these walls to see. Our Heavenly Father was correctly portrayed as an exalted, glorified being of flesh and bone, possessing a tangible body in whose image we, His children, are made. One wonders how else could He be portrayed?

Ask any young child, innocent and untainted by the philosophies of the world, to draw a picture of God, our Heavenly Father, and undoubtedly he or she will draw an image similar to the one that I saw on the ceiling of Sacre Coeur. That is what little children inherently think of when they try to envision their Heavenly Father, for the Spirit whispers to their hearts that they are truly made in His image.

This is another doctrine concerning the true nature of God that led me to my conversion to the LDS Church. Latter-day Saints believe that "the Father has a body of flesh and bones as tangible as man's; the Son also; but the Holy Ghost has not a body of flesh and bones, but is a personage of Spirit" (Doctrine and Covenants 130:22). Latter-day Saints do not believe in a God that is without body, form, or substance, that is, an immaterial spirit essence which fills the immensity of the universe. In their desire to truly know God, Latter-day Saints believe it is important to understand the distinction between these two concepts of our Heavenly Father.

MADE IN THE IMAGE OF GOD

Let us turn again to the scriptures to learn what the prophets, who know God firsthand, have to say on this matter. In the book of Genesis, Moses teaches that God made man in His own image and likeness (Genesis 1:26; 5:1). While those who might be offended by the thought of God in bodily form argue that this scripture refers only to God's "moral" image, this interpretation is in no way substantiated by the balance of holy writ.

It is curious that some would believe that while in mortality a corruptible, sinful man can be in the same "moral" image as the Almighty God who is incorruptible, sinless, in short, morally perfect. Are we to believe that we currently enjoy the same moral character that our Heavenly Father possesses? Or that we observe the same moral standards as Him? The fact is that some men and women, refusing to repent of their sins or exercise faith in God, will never overcome their sinful, immoral nature.[1] How can they profess to be in the "moral" image of God?

Others profess that man is made in the "spiritual" image of God. The Latter-day Saints would concur with this interpretation. We are made in both the spiritual and physical image of God. Our spiritual and physical bodies share similar form, yet are different in substance, as will be discussed shortly.

A further reading of the Genesis account reveals that Adam "begat a son in his own likeness, after his image; and called his name Seth" (Genesis 5:3). The similarities that existed between God and Adam also existed between Adam and Seth. Limiting these similarities to their moral or spiritual image is scripturally unjustified. Rather, physical image and likeness must be included if the scripture is to be interpreted correctly in light of all other scripture. In other words, the whole man, physical and spiritual, is created in God's image.

Many Old Testament prophets have testified to the physical and personal nature of God. Before receiving the stone tablets on which the Ten Commandments were inscribed, Moses, accompanied by Aaron, Nadab, Abihu, and seventy elders of Israel, *saw the God of Israel:* and there was under his *feet* as it were a paved work of a sapphire stone" (Exodus 24:9-11). God later "spake unto Moses *face to face,* as a man speaketh unto his friend" (Exodus 33:11). The biblical author was very clear here in his choice of words, thus relating an event in a manner we can easily understand. Lest we mistakenly believe the language to be figurative, he uses imagery that conveys an accurate picture in our minds, there being only one way that a man could have spoken to his friend "face to face."

Later, in the same chapter of Exodus, the Lord said to Moses, "Behold, there is a place by me, and thou shalt stand upon a rock: And it shall come to pass, while my glory passeth by, that I will put thee in a clift of the rock, and will cover thee with my *hand* while I pass by: And I will take away mine *hand,* and thou shalt see my *back parts:* but my *face* shall not be seen" (Exodus 33:21-23). In this scripture, God mentioned His hand, face, and back, hardly the attributes of a being without body, parts, or form.

THE SON MADE IN THE LIKENESS OF THE FATHER

Just as the Old Testament prophets testified of God's physical appearances, witnessing the glory of His person, so too did the Savior Himself and other New Testament personalities speak in clear terms of the Father's corporeal nature. Christ taught his disciples, "And he that seeth me seeth him that sent me" (John 12:45), meaning that He is the perfect revelation of the Father. The Son is like the Father in all respects, including physical appearance. Christ was sent in behalf of His Father to do and say all that the Father would have done and said in like circumstances.

To further emphasize this point, the apostle Paul taught that the Father has spoken to us by his Son, who is the "express image of his person" (Hebrews 1:1-3). The terminology "express image" comes from the Greek word, "charakter," which means the "mark" of an engraving tool. The engraving tool can produce a stamped likeness or an exact reproduction of itself on the artisan's chosen medium while maintaining its distinct physical identity. Likewise, the Son possesses the "stamp" or "mark" of his Father's divinity and exact physical form while maintaining His own separate identity.[2] The Father and the Son are similar in all their divine attributes, spiritual and physical alike. The Son now possesses a perfect, glorified body of flesh and bone (Luke 24:39), similar to that of His Father. If it were not so, then Christ could not be "in the *form* of God" (Philippians 2:6).

Immediately prior to Stephen's stoning, he was granted a rare glimpse of heaven, seeing "the Son of man [Jesus Christ] standing on the right hand of God" (Acts 7:56). Stephen saw one being standing on the right hand of another, clearly indicating that the Father had a form next to which the Son could stand. The Savior was standing on the "right hand" of His Father, as opposed to the left, as a symbolic gesture of His divine power, authority, and righteousness.

Paul also stated that the Son "is the image of the invisible God" (Colossians 1:15). The word "image" translates into the Greek term, "eikon," which is the same term that the Savior used in referring to Caesar's picture on a Roman coin (Matthew 22:20). Just as the "image" on the coin was a physical likeness of Caesar, the Son is a physical likeness of His Father. The same word is used in the Greek Old Testament when God is said to have created man "in his own image" (Genesis 1:27).[3] Clearly, the scriptures teach that the Father, His beloved Son, and each of His spirit children share the same "image." To ignore the physical aspects of this "image" is to ignore the context within which this term is used throughout the scriptures.

Those who reject the physical nature of the Father are faced with the dilemma as to which is more perfect — an immaterial Father or a material Christ — for the notion of perfection presupposes that any deviation from the ideal state or condition is less than perfection. If the immaterial Father is perfect, then it must follow that the flesh-and-bone Son is less than perfect.

Misunderstood Teachings Concerning God's Nature

With so many biblical accounts of firsthand sightings of God's physical form, why do so many of His children continue to insist that He is a formless, immaterial, ethereal essence which permeates all creation — being everywhere at once, but in no one place in particular? This sort of being hardly fits the description of the loving, personal Father that Christ teaches us to emulate.

Certain biblical scriptures have been misinterpreted and taken out of context to promote the belief in an intangible God. The apostle John wrote, "No man hath seen God at any time" (John 1:18, 1 John 4:12), and Moses quoted God as saying, "No man can see my face" (Exodus 33:20). Does this imply that God has no body (or face), or that God has a body yet no man is allowed to see it? If I told you that you can't see my face, would you infer from my statement that I don't have a face, or that my face is simply hidden from view?

We have already discussed certain scriptural accounts in which chosen men have seen God "face to face" (Exodus 33:11). Why then the contradiction? The answer lies in the following statement made by Christ: "Not that any man hath seen the Father, save *he which is of God, he hath seen the Father*" (John 6:44-46). Only those who are "of God" can see the Father. And who is "of God?" The Apostle John, writing to members of the Church, declared, "He that doeth good is *of God:* but *he that doeth evil hath not seen God*" (3 John 1:11). Only those that God has chosen as worthy and righteous men of faith, such as Moses, have seen him. The Savior also taught that the angels in heaven "do always behold the *face of my Father* which is in heaven" (Matthew 18:10). Nevertheless, those who are carnal and unrighteous, forsaking his commandments, are not worthy to look upon the Almighty God.

The Apostle Paul mentioned the "invisible" nature of God when he wrote, "In whom we have redemption through his [Christ's] blood, even the forgiveness of sins: Who is the image of the *invisible* God [the Father]" (Colossians 1:14-15). Like his colleague, John, Paul also understood the prerequisite to seeing God. God is "invisible," or as the word would be better rendered, "unseen," to man in general, yet he is not "invisible" to righteous and worthy individuals, such as the holy prophets.[4] It was by faith, Paul wrote to the Hebrews, that Moses was able to look upon God, "seeing him who is invisible" (Hebrews 11:27). Clearly, in this context, the word "invisible" is figurative.

Another scripture which is frequently used in an effort to argue for God's nonphysical nature states that "God is not a man" (Numbers 23:19). A more complete reading reveals the intended message this biblical author hoped to convey. "God is not a man, that he should lie; neither the son of man, that he should repent: hath he said, and shall not do it? or hath he spoken, and shall he not make it good?" The obvious point to be made is that, unlike man, God always keeps His promises. No inference to physical nature was intended.

Still another scripture often taken out of context is found in the Book of Jeremiah: "Can any hide himself in secret places that I shall not see him? saith the Lord. Do not I fill heaven and earth? saith the Lord" (Jeremiah 23:24). The implication is made by some that God's essence fills the universe, as a literal interpretation is wrongfully applied. Actually, the Lord is exclaiming the futility of trying to conceal our wicked thoughts or deeds from Him, for He sees all and knows all.

How does God "fill heaven and earth?" The Lord's glory fills the universe, just as "the glory of the Lord filled the tabernacle" erected by the ancient Israelites (Exodus 40:34), or as "all the earth shall be filled with the glory of the Lord" (Numbers 14:21). The glory of God is not to be mistaken with the person of God. God's glory usually represents His almighty power and majesty, as seen in Isaiah 6:3, and can even refer to an outward, visible manifestation of the Divine presence, as in Luke 2:9. Thus, it is God's power, glory, and influence which "fills heaven and earth," not His person.

"GOD IS A SPIRIT"

Perhaps the most misunderstood scripture in the Bible is John's statement, "God is a Spirit: and they that worship him must worship him in spirit and in truth" (John 4:24). In some translations, such as the New International Version, this scripture is rendered, "God is spirit." To fully understand this scripture, and more importantly, the true nature of God, it is essential to understand the meaning of "spirit."

What is a "spirit?" Some are tempted to apply their own defin-ition, without any scriptural support, professing that a spirit is formless, shapeless, and immaterial, filling the immensity of the heavens. What do the scriptures reveal relative to the nature of a spirit? When the apostles saw Jesus walking on the Sea of Galilee, they were frightened, saying, "It is a spirit" (Matthew 14:26). When Christ later appeared to his apostles, following His resurrection, again they were frightened "and supposed that they had seen a spirit" (Luke 24:37).

The apostles obviously knew that a spirit was in the form of a man, otherwise they wouldn't have mistaken the Savior for one. With this much established, if God is only a spirit, it is still evident that He would have form similar to that of man's. However, John did not write that God is *only* a spirit; he wrote, "God *is* a Spirit." This should not be confusing since God is a spirit in the same sense that man is a spirit. Modern revelation teaches us that "all spirit is matter, but it is more fine or pure, and can only be discerned by purer eyes; we cannot see it; but when our bodies are purified we shall see that it is all matter" (Doctrine & Covenants 131:7-8).

The Bible is abundant in passages which teach that man is a spirit. The Old Testament scriptures testify that God "formeth the *spirit of man* within him" (Zechariah 12:1), and that "there is a spirit in man" (Job 32:8). The New Testament teaches that God is "the Father of spirits" (Hebrews 12:9), and his "Spirit itself beareth witness with *our spirit,* that we are the children of God" (Romans 8:16). When the Savior used His divine power to raise the daughter of Jairus, He "took her by the hand, and called, saying, Maid arise. And *her spirit* came again, and she arose straightway" (Luke 8:54-55).

Upon mortal death, man's spirit and mortal body are separated, as his body returns to the dust from whence it came and his spirit returns to God (Ecclesiastes 12:7). In the realm of spirits, man's spirit lives on, awaiting the resurrection, which is the reunion of spirit and body. "The body without the spirit is dead" (James 2:26), indicating the very essence of man's being is his spirit.

Man is indeed spirit, or *a* spirit. He is a spirit, yet we do not think of him as a formless, immaterial, ethereal being. Man is a spirit clothed in a tabernacle of clay during this probationary period we call mortal life. God is a spirit in the same sense that man is a spirit, and He, too, is clothed in a tabernacle of flesh and bone. While man possesses an imperfect, corruptible, temporary body of flesh, bone, and blood, our Heavenly Father has a perfect, incorruptible, eternal body of flesh and bone (no blood), similar to the one Christ revealed to his disciples immediately after His resurrection. We, too, await the day when God will "change our vile body, that it may be fashioned like unto his glorious body" (Philippians 3:21).

Again referring to John 4:24, we read that we are to "worship him [God] *in spirit* and in truth." This does not imply that our spirits must leave our bodies in order that we can worship Him "in spirit."[5] In this sense of the word, it is evident that John meant "spirit" to indicate unity, love, righteousness, and the like, for as Paul declared, "He that is joined unto the Lord is one spirit" (1 Corinthians 6:17).

The physical embodiment of God is more readily understood

when it is recognized that unembodied spirits seek and desire physical tabernacles. This fact is evidenced by the Savior's confrontation with a man whose physical body was possessed by a legion of devils or wicked spirits (Matthew 8:28-34; Mark 5:1-19; Luke 8:26-36). When the evil spirits saw the Lord approach them, the possessed man asked, "What have I to do with thee, Jesus, thou Son of God most high? I beseech thee, torment me not" (Luke 8:28). "And Jesus asked him, saying, What is thy name? And he said, Legion: because many devils were entered into him. And they besought him that he would not command them to go out into the deep [or abyss]" (Luke 8:30).

So great was their fear of being cast out of the tormented man's physical body into the horrible emptiness of space that they made a most unusual request: "And there was there an herd of many swine feeding on the mountain: and they besought him that he would suffer them to enter into them. And he suffered them. Then went the devils out of the man, and entered into the swine" (Luke 8:32-33). These wretched, pitiful devils preferred the physical tabernacles of a herd of pigs to the horror and despair they experienced as unembodied spirits, knowing they had forfeited their opportunity of ever possessing physical bodies of their own through their disobedience.

God, an eternal spirit, has chosen to be housed in a glorified, perfect tabernacle of flesh and bone in order to realize a fullness of joy and power. Likewise, He has sent us, His children, to earth to gain physical bodies, among other things, in order that we, too, may begin to experience the fullness of joy that He currently enjoys. When God replaces our imperfect mortal bodies with glorified resurrected bodies, we will be one step closer to making that hope a reality.

LITERALISM VS. FIGURATISM

As many of the preceding scriptures amply illustrate, two totally divergent views of the nature of God can be construed from the same prophetic writings. What the Latter-day Saints interpret literally, others often interpret figuratively, and vice versa. For example, Latter-day Saints believe that man was created in the literal image of God (Genesis 1:26; 5:1-3), while others might appeal to more figurative or allegorical interpretations. Latter-day Saints believe that Christ is in the "express image of his [Father's] person" (Hebrews 1:3), that God really spoke to Moses "face to face, as a man speaketh unto his friend" (Exodus 33:11), and that Stephen actually saw "the Son of man [Jesus Christ] standing on the right hand of God" (Acts 7:56).

From Genesis to Revelation, the ancient prophets clearly recognized God as a personal, interactive, living, loving, caring, tangible person possessing feelings and emotions. Why should anyone find this truth offensive or heretical when their Lord and Savior possesses these very same qualities and characteristics? The Latter-day Saints believe in a tangible, perfect, eternal, glorified, embodied God as has been revealed to man in the Lord Jesus Christ. Is not Jesus both God and man? Does He not have a body? Will He ever relinquish his glorified body? Is His body somehow abhorrent? The divinity and resurrection of Jesus Christ testify of the doctrine of an exalted, physical God.

Literal interpretations of the Bible are typically refuted with references to biblical passages which are clearly figurative, somehow implying that the existence of some figurative language in the scriptures precludes literal interpretation of other biblical passages. For example, the Psalmist wrote, "He [the Lord] shall cover thee with his feathers, and under his wings shalt thou trust" (Psalms 91:4). Christ used similar language when he said, "How often would I have gathered thy children together, even as a hen gathereth her chickens under her wings, and ye would not" (Matthew 23:37). In these two passages, figurative language is used to highlight the Lord's love and care for His children. The prophets often describe God in figurative language in order to emphasize some particular divine characteristic.

In other passages, he is likened to a rock (Deuteronomy 32:4; 2 Samuel 22:2; 1 Corinthians 10:4) to emphasize his steadfastness, or to a fire (Deuteronomy 4:24) to stress his potential wrath. John the Beloved Apostle wrote, "He that loveth not knoweth not God; for God is love" (1 John 4:8). Obviously, God is more than an emotion or feeling, yet John stresses God's pure and infinite love for his children by simply stating, "God is love."

Clearly, these scriptures are not to be taken literally; however, they are often used to argue against the doctrine of God's physical nature. The implication is made that Moses did not really speak to God "face to face" or that Stephen did not see the Father and the Son in the literal sense, since other scriptures make figurative references to God's nature. Those advocating an immaterial God use these passages to argue that it is just as ridiculous to picture our Heavenly Father in Christ's form — with arms, legs, head, and torso — as it is to picture Him with feathers or wings.

Latter-day Saints believe that the scriptures are not meant to be interpreted on an entirely literal or figurative basis; there are obviously elements of both forms of expression within the prophetic books of the Bible. Some references to God and His dealings with man should be interpreted literally, while others need to be understood figuratively. With the Holy Spirit as our guide, we can more easily discern the difference.

Latter-day Saints recognize the reality of events such as the parting of the Red Sea, the Flood in Noah's day, Jonah's three-day experience inside a large fish, Adam and Eve eating the forbidden fruit in the Garden of Eden, and the crucifixion and resurrection of Jesus Christ. For Latter-day Saints, these are literal depictions of real events.

On the other hand, when the Savior taught in parables, He spoke allegorically to graphically convey eternal principles or truths to His followers. Likewise, allusions to particular characteristics of God utilizing symbolic language such as the caring hen or the solid rock are also clearly figurative. However, references to God's hands, feet, face, or body are more clearly literal, since the Lord has taught us that we are made in His image, and the Son of God, Jesus Christ, literally possessed such physical characteristics.

The movement away from literal toward an almost universal allegorical interpretation of the sacred writings commenced after the death of the apostolic guardians of the Church in an effort to explain away many of the pure and simple doctrines of Christ's Church, especially the unsophisticated, unphilosophical, anthropomorphic language used by the prophets and apostles.

It should be added that literalizing figurative language can be just as doctrinally dangerous as this practice of allegorizing passages which were meant to be literal. Two previously discussed scriptures amply illustrate this point. In his letter to the Colossians, Paul referred to our Heavenly Father as "the invisible God" (Colossians 1:14-15). In another passage, the prophet Jeremiah quotes the Lord as saying, "Do not I fill heaven and earth" (Jeremiah 23:24). Both of these scriptures, when taken in their proper context and harmonized with other prophetic writings, are clearly figurative expressions of specific characteristics of the Lord. The first refers to the inaccessibility of God to natural, carnal man, while the second emphasizes His awareness of all things transpiring within His creation, as well as His all-encompassing power.

THE APOSTASY AND THE NATURE OF THE FATHER

Just as the teachings of uninspired men were mixed with scriptural truths to pervert the true doctrine of the Godhead, so, too, did they influence the original doctrines relative to the physical nature of the Father. The philosophies of men, particularly those of the ancient Greeks and Gnostics, were largely responsible for the discorporation or disembodiment of God.[6]

The Greek philosopher, Plato, espoused a dualism between the spirit (intellect) and matter. The Greeks, as well as the Gnostics, perceived physical matter as evil and corruptible while spirit was good and incorruptible.[7] This dualism promoted the idea that the pure, immaterial spirit was imprisoned within the defiled flesh during this earthly existence. It was this false belief that gave rise to certain orders of monks and recluses who sought to subdue their physical bodies through extreme ascetic practices of self-denial and -torture in order that their spirits might gain greater freedom.[8]

The influence exerted by Greek philosophers on the Christian faith began to take its toll as more and more Greek converts joined the Church. The offensive Christian anthropomorphism was replaced by Greek intellectualism. "There is one God, greatest among gods and men; neither in appearance nor in mind does he resemble mortals" (Xenophanes). "Since he is eternal and one and equally distributed, he can be neither boundless nor bound, for he has neither center nor definition or any other part" (Xenophanes). "He has no human head or limbs, neither from his back do two arms grow, nor legs, nor trunk nor other parts, but he is sacred, ineffable (indescribable) Mind, filling the whole vast universe with his thoughts" (Empedocles). "Since it is One it can have no corporeal substance; if it were vulnerable it would have parts, and having parts it would not be One" (Melissus).

"It cannot be conceived of as having any size or parts or division, since it is not limited, as every dimension must be, and to be infinite is to have no dimensions" (Aristotle). "He is not like a man or any living thing, he has no body great or small, but is unutterable, indefinable, incomparable, to anything else, divine, alone..." (Plutarch). "The good is the opposite of anything corporeal" (Plutarch). "All matter is evil, there is nothing true or good in it, since it is the opposite of perfect Being" (Plotinus).[9] The similarities between this Hellenistic concept of deity and the popular concept of an immaterial, incomprehensible God recognized since the post-apostolic period are more than mere coincidence.

These Greek and Gnostic teachings had a detrimental effect on the true principles of Christ's gospel, giving birth to the belief that God must be only pure spirit in order to be incorruptible. These false doctrines were able to creep into the Church after the death of the apostles and the resultant cessation of divine revelation. The proponents of this concept of the Eternal Father as an immaterial spirit essence failed to realize that His physical nature in no way rendered

Him corruptible or limited in power.

Latter-day Saints do not believe that the glorious, resurrected body possessed by his Son, Jesus Christ, is corruptible or imperfect, or that it inhibits His almighty power in any way. Likewise, the body possessed by the Father enhances, not lessens, His own greatness and power.

The physical resurrection of Jesus Christ is unequivocal evidence that matter is not evil. Would the Lord take on an eternal, glorified body consisting of physical matter if matter was known to be evil? Actually, it is spirit that shows evil tendencies, as witnessed in the unembodied evil spirits of Satan and his wicked followers. The power of righteousness or wickedness lies within the spirit, not physical matter.

If matter was truly evil as the philosophers would have us believe, then why would God offer us the promise of eternal life in a resurrected body? Also, if God is nonphysical as many believe, then why would God, who has power to do all things and who possesses an infinite love for His children, give us an eternal physical body when He could endow us with a supposedly superior nonphysical spirit essence?

THE OMNIPRESENCE OF GOD

Latter-day Saints do not believe that God must be immaterial for Him to be omnipresent. The omnipresence of God simply refers to the all-pervading power, glory, and influence He exercises through the Holy Spirit and not the ubiquity of His personal being or physical body. He is omnipresent by virtue of the light of Christ "which light proceedeth forth from the presence of God to fill the immensity of space — the light which is in all things, which giveth life to all things, which is the law by which all things are governed" (Doctrine & Covenants 88:11-12).

God is omnipotent in that He can do all things. He is omniscient in that He knows and sees all things. God's personal being does not have to be everywhere for Him to be all-seeing or all-knowing, for His eyes can see beyond the reach of His almighty arm. Just as you or I can see all things transpiring within a room of our own home without our body physically filling its entire airspace, God can see all things throughout His vast universe without filling the immensity of its space with His immediate person or being. As the Psalmist wrote, "The Lord looketh *from heaven*; he beholdeth all the sons of men. *From the place of his habitation* he looketh upon all inhabitants of the earth" (Psalms 33:13-14). The scriptures also reveal that "God is in heaven, and thou [mortal man] upon earth" (Ecclesiastes 5:2).

Clearly, the being or personage of the Lord does not fill the universe, yet as He resides in His heavenly abode, He can see all of His creation.

"WE ARE THE OFFSPRING OF GOD"

Latter-day Saints are not ashamed of their unphilosophical belief in a loving, personal Heavenly Father that possesses a physical body of flesh and bone in whose image man was created. To many people, this might seem foolish, nevertheless "God hath chosen the foolish things of the world to confound the wise" (1 Corinthians 1:27).

Latter-day Saints do not believe that God is some abstract or metaphysical essence or power. They believe He is a very real person. Likewise, He is more than our Creator, as we are more than His creatures. He is the literal Father of our spirits and we are His children (John 20:17; Romans 8:16; Hebrews 12:9).

The Apostle Paul taught that "we are the offspring of God" (Acts 17:29), thus we are made in His image. (La Sainte Bible published by the Alliance Biblique Universelle, a popular French language Bible, translates this passage in the ancient Greek texts to say that we are of the "race of God"). When does the offspring not resemble the parent? Given a formless, immaterial, impersonal God on one hand, and a tangible, personal Heavenly Father whose form and image we resemble on the other, one might ask, "Which God, or which image of the Father, is most worthy and deserving of our child-like love and adoration?"[10]

I know which God is the object of my devotions, for "behold, what manner of love the Father hath bestowed upon us, that we should be called the sons of God: therefore the world knoweth us not, because it knew him not. Beloved, *now are we the sons of God,* and it doth not yet appear what we shall be: but we know that, *when he shall appear, we shall be like him; for we shall see him as he is"* (1 John 3:1-2).

There will come a much-anticipated day after our resurrection, when we shall stand before the throne of Almighty God, our Heavenly Father, and gaze upon the brilliance and magnificence of His glory. Knowing that we will possess glorious and perfect eternal bodies, and knowing that when we see Him "we shall be like Him," it should come as no surprise to His children that the Eternal Father possesses a similar, yet infinitely more glorious, eternal body.

4

THE DOCTRINE OF SALVATION

AS soon as he hit the ball, Jason knew he had gotten all of it with the fattest part of the bat. Jason had been playing baseball in the street in front of his house almost every day since school ended in June, and this undoubtedly was his best hit of the summer. As he watched the trajectory of the long fly ball, his glee quickly turned to dismay as the ball crashed through the large bay window of his neighbor's house. That was the end of the game, and he felt, the end of his life.

Jason thought to himself, "That window is bigger than my whole room. I'll never be able to pay to have it fixed. What am I going to do?" He slowly walked home to tell his mother the bad news, while dreading what his father would do when he came home from work.

Later that evening, when he finally confessed his crime to his father, he was surprised by his father's calm response. "Well, son, it looks like you have quite the problem. I'm sure that window will cost more than all the lemonade you could sell in the next 20 summers. What do you plan to do?"

Jason didn't have any idea how he could pay for his mistake. He was only eight years old, therefore he wasn't old enough to have a paper route. With the allowance he received for doing chores around the house, he figured it would take at least a hundred years to pay Mr. Kelly back for the broken window. He finally responded to his father's inquiry, "I don't know, Dad. Can't you help me?"

Jason's father could detect true remorse and desperation in his son's humble plea. He looked into Jason's sad eyes and said, "I'm sure we can come up with something between the two of us. Let's think about it for awhile."

The next day, when Jason's father returned from work, he called his son into the living room. "Jason, I think I have come up with a workable plan which will allow us to pay your debt to Mr. Kelly. It is a plan that involves an element of justice and an element of mercy. Regarding the mercy part of this arrangement, I will agree to pay for the cost of fixing Mr. Kelly's window, since I know you have no way of paying for it yourself.

"Now, for the justice part, Mr. Kelly will be fully reimbursed for his broken window, but I will place a condition upon my payment of your debt. I want you to learn a lesson from your mistake. I also want you to do everything within your power to correct this situation. If you agree to my terms, I will pay your debt to Mr. Kelly."

Jason's eyes lit up, "You bet, Dad. I'll do anything."

His father continued, "If you will take out the garbage every day, clean your room every day, and be kind to your little sister, in addition to all of your other chores, then I think we have a deal."

Jason knew these were conditions he could meet. "You've got a deal, Dad." He also knew he was getting off easy. He was elated to have a way to get out of his seemingly inescapable predicament. Jason hugged his father and added with a smile, "Being nice to my sister is going to be the tough part."

What his father had asked of him was but a small price to pay for relief from his monumental and otherwise unpayable debt. He knew that he couldn't pay the debt himself, nor could he repay his father. But, in his love and compassion, his father agreed to assume his debt in return for his compliance to a few house rules. While the rules were challenging, they were achievable. And they did serve a purpose. Submission to his father's conditions would allow him to demonstrate his true remorse for his mistake, express his love and gratitude to his father for his generosity, and develop the righteous character attributes of obedience, industry, and kindness, all of which would inevitably make him a better person.

This modern-day parable illustrates the LDS perspective of the atoning sacrifice of Jesus Christ in simple and understandable terms. Just as Jason had broken a window for which he could not pay, all of us, as children of God, have broken eternal laws, through sin, for which we cannot pay. And just as Jason's father intervened on his behalf, our Savior, Jesus Christ, has volunteered to pay the price of sin on our behalf. While Jason's father expected mere compliance with a few household chores and rules of behavior in return for his generosity, so, too, does our Lord expect from us obedience to His reasonable and do-able commandments in return for His divine intermediation.

The teachings of the Latter-day Saints regarding the plan of salvation for God's children stand as one more reason for my spiritual conversion. Latter-day Saints do not believe the popular doctrine that man is saved by the grace of God alone, or that God requires no effort on man's part to qualify for eternal life. According to this belief, a simple lip confession or internal acknowledgment of one's faith in Jesus Christ as his personal Savior is all that is necessary to qualify the individual for God's grace and thereby inherit eternal life in God's kingdom. Latter-day Saints believe this teaching discourages any or all motivation to repent, obey, and grow spiritually, since it does not require any change in the individual's lifestyle or behavior.

It is commonly thought by others that as Latter-day Saints we do not believe in the grace of God, but instead believe that we are saved by our works. This is another misconception that others harbor concerning the doctrine of the Latter-day Saints. In actuality, we believe that eternal salvation is attained by virtue of both the grace of God and works of righteous obedience. Both are essential; one is not a substitute for the other.

THE GRACE OF GOD

In order to better understand this concept, we need to define some terms, beginning with "grace." The grace of God consists in the Almighty's love, mercy, and condescension toward his children. All things that exist for the benefit of man are manifestations of God's grace.[1]

Relative to man's salvation, grace refers to that which Jesus Christ has done for us that we could not possibly have done for ourselves. First, He created this earth upon which we live and gain experience (Colossians 1:16-17). Second, He atoned for the trans-gression of Adam and Eve, which introduced physical death into the world, thus bringing to pass the universal resurrection from the grave (1 Corinthians 15:22; John 5:28-29). Third, He has given us all the opportunity to attain eternal life, which is to live in the presence of God throughout eternity, by atoning for our personal sins upon conditions of repentance (Hebrews 5:9).

These are free gifts of God without which all mankind would be lost forever; nevertheless, His provisions of grace in no way excuse us of our responsibility to obey His commandments. He has paid the debt for our sins, now we must satisfy the terms of His gracious inter-vention on our behalf by repenting of (turning away from) our sins and obeying His commandments in order to become benefactors of His atoning sacrifice. The Savior has provided the means by which we may "work out [our] own salvation" (Philippians 2:12) by virtue of His power and grace. He has provided the way to salvation and we must now follow it, "because strait is the gate, and narrow is the way, which leadeth unto life, and few there be that find it" (Matthew 7:14).

SALVATION: UNIVERSAL AND INDIVIDUAL

It is also expedient to define the term "salvation." I found that salvation conjures up different ideas for different people of different faiths, and often those within the same faith. The prophets have revealed that there are two distinct types of salvation. The first is salvation from physical death, or salvation from the effects of the sin of Adam, which is unconditional and universal, meaning it applies to all mankind regardless of the individual's beliefs or actions. This is made possible through the grace of Jesus Christ, our Savior, who overcame the sting of physical death for all, both the just and the unjust, by virtue of His physical resurrection (1 Corinthians 15:22; John 5:28-29; Luke 3:6). In short, all mankind will be resurrected.

The second type is salvation from spiritual death, or salvation from our own personal sins, which is conditional and individual. (Spiritual death is to be cast out of the presence of God, that is, to be separated from God and the things of righteousness). This type of salvation, also known as exaltation, is also made possible through the grace of Jesus Christ and is offered to all mankind by way of His infinite atoning sacrifice. This salvation requires individual effort in the form of faith in Jesus Christ, repentance of personal sins, obedience to the commandments and ordinances of the gospel, and continued righteous living until the very end of our mortal lives. If we desire the Savior to save us from the adverse effects of our personal sins, we must be willing and able to turn away from those sins, for Jesus Christ is truly "the author of eternal salvation *unto all them that obey him*" (Hebrews 5:9).

This is consistent with biblical teachings as previously offered scriptural references have shown and as subsequent references will continue to show. The Savior taught, "I am the *resurrection,* and the *life*" (John 11:25). In a letter to Timothy, Paul wrote that Christ's atoning sacrifice "abolished death, and hath brought life and immortality to light through the gospel" (2 Timothy 1:10). Through the Savior's atonement comes the resurrection, which is immortality or the opposite of physical death, as well as eternal life, which is immortality in God's kingdom or the antithesis of spiritual death.

The resurrected Lord declared to the Apostle John, "I am he that liveth, and was dead; and, behold, I am alive for evermore, Amen; and have the keys of hell [spiritual death] and of death [physical death]" (Revelation 1:18). The Savior holds the "keys," or power and authority over physical and spiritual death, by virtue of His resurrection and eternal atoning sacrifice. Salvation from physical death (immortality) is attained solely by the grace of God, whereas salvation from spiritual death (eternal life or exaltation) is achieved through both God's grace and obedience to His commandments. In other words, we are saved by grace and exalted by grace and works.

JUDGED BY WORKS

The essentiality of righteous works becomes readily apparent when one considers the matter of the final judgement. The scriptures teach us "that there shall be a resurrection of the dead, both of the just and unjust" (Acts 24:15), therefore all mankind will be saved from physical death. Yet this does not mean that all men will live in God's kingdom in His glorious presence. All mankind will be resurrected, "for we must all appear before the judgment seat of Christ; that everyone may receive the things done in his body, according to that he hath done, whether it be good or bad" (2 Corinthians 5:10).

John the Revelator was given the privilege of witnessing in vision the great day of judgment, wherein all of God's children stood before their Creator and "they were judged everyman according to their works" (Revelation 20:12-13; Matthew 16:27). He learned by divine revelation that every man and woman will be judged according to his or her works in order to determine their place of eternal residence, whether it be in God's kingdom or elsewhere.

Notice that these scriptures make no reference to a simple lip confession or passive internal acknowledgment of one's faith in Christ as being adequate to inherit eternal life. We will be judged according to our actions, in addition to our words and thoughts, making good works requisite to entering God's kingdom. As for those committed to lip service rather than true service, the Lord has declared, "This people draw near me with their mouth, and with their lips do honour me, but have removed their heart far from me" (Isaiah 29:13).

Initially, the notion of "justification by faith alone" was an extension of the false doctrine of predestination. Toward the close of the Dark Ages, some religious reformers claimed that all of mankind's actions were the predetermined will of God. It was Martin Luther who incorrectly taught the following: "The excellent, infallible, and sole preparation for grace, is the eternal election and predestination of God." "Since the fall of man, freewill is but an idle word." "A man who imagines to arrive at grace by doing all that he is able to do, adds sin to sin, and is doubly guilty."[2] This concept of salvation implied that since man was stripped of his free will, predestined to act without choice, he was incapable of doing anything that would affect his eternal salvation. The path to heaven or hell was prechosen for him.

Since Luther's time, much of Christendom have wisely rejected this notion of predestination while unwisely clinging to the associated doctrine of justification by faith alone. Many have espoused a position of inconsistency by admitting that man does exercise his free will, choosing between good and evil according to his own volition, while still insisting that his choices and actions have no merit or bear no influence on his eternal destination.

TRUE BELIEF IN CHRIST

A commonly taught doctrine today states that all an individual is required to do to receive eternal life is simply "believe" that Jesus Christ is his personal Savior and confess this in his heart or vocally, and he is then immediately "saved by grace." To support such a doctrine, reference is frequently made to scriptures such as John 3:36 which states, "He that believeth on the Son hath everlasting life," or Romans 1:16 which reads, "For I am not ashamed of the gospel of Christ: for it is the power of God unto salvation to every one that believeth." By appealing solely to these and similar scriptures, the implication is made that true belief does not include individual effort, consequently many other relevant biblical scriptures are not taken into consideration in order to gain a more balanced perspective on the subject of salvation.

It is unwise to separate a single passage of scripture from its proper context in an attempt to force an interpretation which is contrary to or inconsistent with God's intended meaning or message.[3] Such has been the case among those who choose to ignore the Lord's interpretation and definition of sincere "belief."

True belief in Jesus Christ implies much more than simple vocal acceptance or internal acknowledgment that He is the Son of God and Savior of the world. Belief implies total commitment to Christ and His gospel teachings. Belief means acceptance of and obedience to His commandments. Belief consists of accepting the Savior's atonement by repenting of one's sins, being baptized into His Church, receiving the gift of the Holy Ghost (Acts 2:38), and obeying all of His commandments.

Can someone honestly proclaim a belief in Christ without believing in His teachings or obeying His commandments? The individual who claims Christ as his personal Savior, yet lacks obedience, is no better off than the nonbeliever, for if one does not obey the Savior, one does not truly believe in Him. On this matter, Jesus Christ taught,"Not every one that saith unto me, Lord, Lord, shall enter into the kingdom of heaven; *but he that doeth the will of my*

Father which is in heaven" (Matthew 7:21). "Verily, verily, I say unto you, He that *believeth* on me, the *works* that I do shall he do also" (John 14:12), thus true believers will be known by their good works.

Latter-day Saints believe that faith requires action, not apathy or passive observance. We demonstrate our faith in the Lord by obeying His will, not by merely professing inwardly or vocally, "I believe." Our inner faith is made manifest by our external acts of love, charity, and righteous obedience. As it has been said that work is love made visible, it might also be said that righteous works are faith made visible.

Consider a pivotal event in the life of the great ancient patriarch, Abraham. The Lord did not bestow great eternal blessings upon Abraham and his posterity until Abraham proved his worthiness through obedience. It wasn't until Abraham was prepared to offer up the life of his only son, Isaac, that an angel of the Lord declared, "For because thou hast done this thing, and hast not withheld thy son, thine only son; That in blessing I will bless thee, and in multiplying I will multiply thy seed as the stars of the heaven, and as the sand which is upon the sea shore; and thy seed shall possess the gate of his enemies; And in thy seed shall all the nations of the earth be blessed; *because thou hast obeyed my voice*" (Genesis 22:18).

The Apostle James confirms that it was Abraham's outward demonstration of his faith in God through righteous obedience that qualified him for these great blessings. "Was not Abraham our father *justified by works,* when he had offered Isaac his son upon the altar? Seest thou how faith wrought with his works, and *by works was faith made perfect?* And the scripture was fulfilled which saith, Abraham believed God, and it was imputed unto him for right-eousness: and he was called the Friend of God. Ye see then how that *by works a man is justified, and not by faith only*" (James 2:21-24). Through outward obedience to God's commandments, it was demonstrated that "Abraham believed God."

The Apostle James further taught that true belief implied much more than mental or vocal confession of Christ as the Savior when he wrote, "Thou believest that there is one God; thou doest well: *the devils also believe,* and tremble. But wilt thou know, O vain man, that *faith without works is dead?*" (James 2:19-20). Even the devils "believe" that Jesus Christ is the Son of God, yet we can be sure that this "belief" does not elicit the power of salvation due to the disobe-dient and wicked nature of these rebellious spirits. Clearly, belief is not enough; it must be accompanied by repentance of personal sins and obedience to the will of God.

Simple belief unaccompanied by works of faith and obedience is powerless to render Christ's atonement operational in our lives. This belief must motivate us to live righteously and obey the gospel, for God will take vengeance on those "that obey not the gospel of our Lord Jesus Christ" (2 Thessalonians 1:8).

"Are You Saved?"

The question is often posed by modern-day believers, "Are you saved?" One might respond by asking, "Saved from what?" Is the believer saved from physical death? Although Paul taught that all must die before passing from this mortal life (1 Corinthians 15:22), we know that all mankind will eventually be resurrected, and in this sense all will ultimately be saved from physical death. However, this is rarely the meaning of salvation that the inquisitor intended.

Is the believer saved from sin? Perhaps he is saved from past sins, if he has fulfilled the Savior's requirements of true repentance. However, James wrote, "To him that knoweth to do good, and doeth it not, to him it is sin" (James 4:17). Due to our weaknesses and imperfections, repentance tends to be a continual lifetime process and not a one-time event.

Unless one has personally received the promise of eternal life, for various reasons it is not truly proper to speak of salvation as an existing condition that we currently enjoy while we continue to abide in our mortal state. First, the Father has designated the Savior to be the Judge of all mankind. Only He can decide who is saved. When an individual professes to be saved, he or she is relinquishing Christ of the sacred task He has been appointed to perform.

Second, an individual who is currently on the straight and narrow path might stray from the course leading to eternal life at some future time. That is, like Judas and others, one might follow the Savior today, yet deny him tomorrow. The scriptures clearly expose the fallacy of the popular belief that man is "once saved, always saved."

Third, in the true and ultimate sense of the word, eternal salvation refers to life in our Heavenly Father's kingdom as a resurrected being. Since no mortal being currently enjoys this status, few are justified in claiming to be "saved." Someone might be on a course leading to salvation, but it is yet a future, not present, condition.

"Keep My Commandments"

No modern-day Christian can rightly deny that God has given

His children commandments. Upon Mount Sinai, Moses received the Ten Commandments that he and all of the House of Israel were to observe. During his Sermon on the Mount, the Savior delineated in great detail a number of commandments of an order higher than those received by Moses. The Savior later declared, "If ye love me, keep my commandments...*He that hath my commandments, and keepeth them, he it is that loveth me: and he that loveth me shall be loved of my Father,* and I will love him, and will manifest myself to him" (John 14:15,21).

Would God give us commandments if He didn't expect or require us to obey them? Is obedience to God's commandments optional? If salvation can be attained without obedience to God's commandments, what is the point of giving them and what is to keep man from following the easier path of disobedience? Perhaps all of our Heavenly Father's children would be unified in their responses to these important questions if they all understood His purpose for giving us commandments.

Our Father gives us commandments in order to encourage us to do good, to test our faithfulness, to show us the way to true happiness, and to prepare us for entrance into His holy kingdom. Obedience to His commandments has a sanctifying or purifying effect on our souls. Simply put, we become better people as we follow Christ's righteous example, thus allowing God's Spirit the opportunity to cleanse our souls. If we fail to obey the commandments of God, we offend the Holy Spirit, who then withdraws from us, and we deprive ourselves of this sanctifying process. The Lord still provides us the means to obtain forgiveness when we make mistakes, but true repentance requires obedience as well as godly sorrow.

If we disobey His commandments after having received and understood them, we have committed sin and have rendered ourselves unclean. As previously stated, James taught, "Therefore to him that knoweth to do good, and doeth it not, to him it is sin" (James 4:17). What will become of the unrepentant sinner, that is, the individual who continues his sinful behavior even after hearing the gospel? Christ offered the answer in his statement, "Whosoever committeth sin is the servant of sin" (John 8:34). Using stronger language, John said, "He that committeth sin is of the devil" (1 John 3:8). And finally, Isaiah revealed the ultimate destiny of those who disobey God's commandments, declaring that at his second coming Christ "shall destroy the sinners" (Isaiah 13:9). Once again, who are the "sinners?" They are those that "knoweth to do good, and doeth it not." While destruction awaits the disobedient, the righteous and obedient may take solace in the fact that "he that *doeth* the will of God abideth forever" (1 John 2:17), and "he that *keepeth his command-ments* dwelleth in him" (1 John 3:24).

LIP SERVICE VS. TRUE SERVICE

Is it just to grant eternal life to a person who professes to "believe" in the Lord yet fails to observe the Savior's command-ments and repent of his personal sins, while giving the same reward to one who has demonstrated his love for the Savior by diligently obeying His commandments? This question is best answered by the Savior's Parable of Two Sons. In this parable, the Lord demon-strated the insufficiency of lip service and the necessity of real obedience. "A certain man had two sons; and he came to the first, and said, Son, go work today in my vineyard.

"He answered and said, I will not: but afterward he repented, and went.

"And he came to the second, and said likewise. And he answered and said, I go, sir: and went not.

"Whether of them twain did the will of his father? They say unto him, The first. Jesus saith unto them [the Jewish religious leaders], Verily I say unto you, That the publicans and the harlots go into the kingdom of God before you" (Matthew 21:28-32).

The son who was deemed worthy to live in our Heavenly Father's kingdom initially said he would not do the will of his father, yet later repented of his disobedience. In contrast to the peni-tent son, the second son said he would fulfill his father's command, but his obedience and respect were no more than hollow promises as he neglected to honor his father in deed. He rendered nothing more than lip service. The Savior taught that it is the first son, that is, the obedient son, that is worthy of entering the Father's kingdom.

The Savior's message is timeless. If we feign righteousness in our pious speech, like the ancient Pharisees, and neglect to worship and honor the Lord in deed, we will fall short of eternal glory. Those who have chosen a course of wickedness, like the publicans and harlots, but have subsequently repented of their evil ways and aligned themselves with the Lord's divine will, shall inherit a place in the kingdom of God. The moral of the Parable of the Two Sons is that true belief in Jesus Christ which leads to salvation requires more than lip service or feigned devotion such as was practiced by the Pharisees. It requires active obedience.

While teaching great gospel doctrines to the multitudes gathered to hear him at the temple in Jerusalem, the Savior explained wherein the Pharisees fell short of God's saving grace. He urged the people to continue to observe whatsoever the Pharisees required, "but do not ye after their works: for *they say, and do not*" (Matthew 23:2-3). Just as the disobedient son in the Parable of the Two Sons said to his father, "I go, sir: and went not" (Matthew 21:30), the Pharisees "say, and do not." They pretended to praise and worship God with their lofty speech and hypocritical behavior, but in reality they practiced the works of darkness, wickedness, and deceit, instead of obeying the commandments of God.

The Pharisees gave a semblance of holiness in their wordy public prayers, pretentious attire, and meticulous observance of hundreds of useless and burdensome religious regulations which they themselves devised, "but all their works they do for to be seen of men" (Matthew 23:5). While fulfilling the letter of the law, they failed to observe the spirit of the law. "Woe unto you, scribes and Pharisees, hypocrites! for ye pay tithe of mint and anise and cummin, and have omitted the weightier matters of the law, judgment, mercy, and faith: these ought ye to have done, and not to leave the other undone" (Matthew 23:23). They did well to pay their tithes, however, they neglected to exercise true Christ-like charity towards their fellowman. They were guilty of seeking the praise of men (Matthew 23:5-7), taking widows' homes (Matthew 23:14), practicing greed, extortion, and self-indulgence at the expense of others (Matthew 23:25), and rejecting the prophets of God (Matthew 23:29-37).

The Savior condemned the Pharisees for their false righteousness and counterfeit obedience: "Even so ye also outwardly appear righteous unto men, but within ye are full of hypocrisy and iniquity" (Matthew 23:28). They disobeyed the commandments of God while burdening their followers with a proliferation of useless legalistic details. The Lord railed, "Howbeit in vain do they worship me, teaching for doctrines the commandments of men.

"For laying aside the commandment of God, ye hold the tradition of men, as the washing of pots and cups: and many other such like things ye do.

"And he said unto them, Full well *ye reject the commandments* of God, that ye may keep your own tradition" (Mark 7:7-9).

The blessings of heaven are predicated upon true righteousness and Christ-like obedience. "And whatsoever we ask, we receive of him, *because we keep his commandments*, and do those things that are pleasing in his sight" (1 John 3:22). The Savior taught his disciples, "For I say unto you, That except your righteousness shall exceed the righteousness of the scribes and Pharisees, ye shall in no case enter into the kingdom of heaven" (Matthew 5:20). The Lord denounced the Pharisees and their followers for their disobedience to His holy commandments, a disobedience which would eternally bar them from His heavenly realm. He taught His disciples that the godly righteousness which leads to eternal life comes from both the heart and the hands as we endeavor to obey our Heavenly Father's will out of love for Him and His children.

CHRIST'S ATONEMENT FOR THE OBEDIENT

Biblical scripture plainly teaches that the Savior requires obedience of us if we are to qualify for the cleansing power of His atoning sacrifice. He will save us *from* our sins upon conditions of repentance, but we are foolish to think He will save us *in* our sins if we fail to turn away from them. "For if we sin wilfully after that we have received the knowledge of the truth [the gospel of Jesus Christ], there remaineth *no more sacrifice for sins*, But a certain fearful looking for of judgment and fiery indignation" (Hebrews 10:26). If we continue in our sinful ways after accepting the Savior and His gospel, we forfeit our claim on His redeeming sacrifice.

"For it had been better for [us] not to have known the way of righteousness, then, after [we] have known it, to turn from the holy commandment delivered unto [us]" (2 Peter 2:21). "But *if we walk in the light*, as he is in the light, we have fellowship one with another, and the blood of Jesus Christ his Son cleanseth us from all sin" (1 John 1:7). To qualify for the cleansing power of Christ's blood we must "walk in the light," which is to say, we must have faith in Christ, we must be actively engaged in good Christian works, and we must be obedient to Christ's commandments (Ephesians 2:10; 1 Thessalonians 4:1-2; 2 John 1:6). "And hereby we do know that we know him, *if we keep his commandments. He that saith, I know him, and keepeth not his commandments, is a liar*, and the truth is not in him" (1 John 2:4-5).

What of those who declare that they believe in Jesus Christ, yet neglect to live righteously and obey all His commandments? "They profess that they know God; but in works they deny him, being abominable, and disobedient, and unto every good work reprobate" (Titus 1:16). Surely there are many who declare Jesus Christ as their Savior, yet trample His commandments under their feet. What is their fate, or as Peter poses the question, "What shall the end be of them that obey not the gospel of God? And if the righteous scarcely be saved, where shall the ungodly and the sinner appear" (1 Peter 4:17-18)?

We can almost hear the voice of Paul as he responds, "Know ye not that the unrighteous shall not inherit the kingdom of God" (1 Corinthians 6:9)? Paul then categorizes many of the unrighteous: fornicators, idolators, adulterers, abusers of themselves [homosexuals], thieves, covetous people, drunkards, revilers, and extortioners, to name a few (1 Corinthians 6:9-10). John even includes liars among the ranks of the wicked who "shall have their part in the lake which burneth with fire and brimstone: which is the second death" (Revelation 21:8).

The Bible is indeed replete with scriptures that declare the necessity of good works, that is, righteousness and obedience, in order to obtain salvation from individual sins and to secure residence in God's holy kingdom. "Let us hear the conclusion of the whole matter: Fear God, and keep his commandments: for this is the whole duty of man. For God shall bring every work into judgment, with every secret thing, whether it be good, or whether it be evil" (Ecclesiastes 12:13-14).

"My mother and my brethren are these which hear the word of God, and do it" (Luke 8:21).

"And, why call ye me, Lord, Lord, and do not the things which I say?" (Luke 6:46).

"But be ye doers of the word, and not hearers only, deceiving your own selves" (James 1:22).

"Be not deceived; God is not mocked: for whatsoever a man soweth, that shall he also reap" (Galatians 6:7). If we think God will save us from our sins and allow us to live in His glorious kingdom without requiring us to obey His commandments, we are indeed deceiving ourselves unto our own damnation.

"What doth it profit, my brethren, though a man say he hath faith, and have not works? Can faith save him? For as the body without the spirit is dead, so faith without works is dead also" (James 2:14,26). (Also read the Parable of the Sower [Matthew 13:3-9] and the Parable of the Entrusted Talents [Matthew 25:14-30]).

What a great privilege it would be to approach the Savior himself and ask Him personally what we must do in order to be assured a place in the kingdom of our Heavenly Father. During Christ's mortal ministry, a certain young, rich man did just that, inquiring of the Lord, "Good Master, what good thing shall I do, that I may have eternal life?" The Lord's response is equally applicable to each of us. "Why callest thou me good? there is none good but one, that is, God: but *if thou wilt enter into life, keep the commandments.*" The young man then asked the Savior which commandments he should observe, to which the Lord replied by enumerating several of the Ten Commandments. When the man insisted that he was already keeping these commandments, the Savior said, "If thou wilt be perfect, go and sell that thou hast, and give to the poor, and thou shalt have treasure in heaven: and come and follow me" (Matthew 19:16-21). The Lord's final statement to the rich man indicates the real commitment and sacrifice associated with true discipleship.

MISUNDERSTOOD TEACHINGS ON SALVATION

The popular doctrine that we are saved by grace alone despite our actions is usually based on a few of Paul's statements, taken out of historical context, regarding the issues of faith, works, and salvation. It is imperative to note that many of Paul's writings are difficult to understand, since they were written for a different time and circumstance. Most of his epistles were written in response to specific problems or questions that arose in certain geographical areas of the first-century Church, and as a result, these epistles offer us only bits and pieces of a much wider range of gospel doctrines and issues. Paul also wrote to Church members whom he presumed already possessed a knowledge of general gospel doctrines, therefore many gospel principles and practices are only alluded to and not fully explained.[4]

Today, the New Testament is commonly used as a "handbook" or "manual" of gospel teachings in an effort to establish a doctrinal foundation or theological system of beliefs, thus employing Paul's writings, along with the other New Testament writings, for a purpose in which they were never intended. Since Paul was not specifically writing with twentieth-century readers in mind, it is not uncommon for modern readers of the Bible to misinterpret Paul's comments by taking his teachings out of their historical context. In other words, present-day students of Bible often lack the complete cultural and doctrinal backdrop that Paul's original audience enjoyed.

In addition, Paul conveyed his responses by both written epistle and "word of mouth" as he traveled throughout the Mediterranean region (2 Thessalonians 2:15), therefore much of his doctrinal dialogue with these early Church branches was never recorded. In essence, the epistles are mere snapshots in time; they are small patches of a much grander tapestry of gospel teachings.

That the apostles taught much which was never recorded as scripture is revealed in one of the oldest surviving fragments of early Christian literature. The following passage comes to us from Clement of Rome, a first-century Christian bishop, as preserved by the second-century Christian Church historian, Eusebius: "The only power they [the Apostles] ever made use of was the assurance of the Holy Ghost and the miraculous power of Christ operating through them, by which they preached the kingdom of God throughout the world. *They gave little thought of writing anything down.* What they did, they did with the aid of a power beyond that of men. Paul, for example, the most skillful speaker and the best educated man of them all, *left nothing in writing but a few extremely short letters;* yet he was in a position to *utter marvelous things without number,* as one having actually been in contact with visions of the third heaven, caught up even to God's paradise, where he was deemed worthy to hear unutterable things. But the other disciples of our Savior were not without experience of these things, either: the twelve Apostles, the Seventy disciples, and countless others under their instruction."[5]

Given the fact that Paul's letters address specific first-century questions and do not teach general doctrines in their entirety, and given the fact that he was writing to an audience already familiar with the general doctrines of the Church, it is easier to understand why Paul's letters are frequently misinterpreted today. In fact, Paul's writing style even led to much confusion in his own time. Realizing this, Peter informed the early Christians, "And account that the long-suffering of our Lord is salvation; even as our beloved brother Paul also according to the wisdom given unto him hath written unto you; As also in all his epistles, speaking in them of these things; in which are some things *hard to be understood,* which they that are unlearned and unstable wrest [twist or distort], as they do also the other scriptures, unto their own destruction" (2 Peter 3:15-16).

Among those scriptures which are often "hard to be understood" is the following: "For by grace are ye saved through faith; and that not of yourselves: it is the gift of God: Not of works, lest any man should boast" (Ephesians 2:8-9). How do we reconcile this with the various scriptures which declare that Heavenly Father's children will be "judged every man according to their works" (Revelation 20:12-13; Matthew 16:27; 2 Corinthians 5:10)? The key to properly interpreting Paul's statement is to identify the historical context and cultural conditions within which it was made. In other words, to whom was Paul specifically writing this letter, and when and why did he write it?

The year was approximately A.D. 61.[6] Paul was writing "to the saints [Church members] which [were] at Ephesus" (Ephesians 1:1), many of whom were recently converted to Christianity from Judaism. During this period, it was heatedly debated throughout the Church whether or not new converts were to continue to observe the Law of Moses which had heretofore played a profound part in Jewish daily life. Many Jews who were converted to Christianity still believed that salvation came through the works of the Mosaic Law, while the apostles, Paul in particular, tried to convince them that the Law of Moses was fulfilled in Christ's atoning sacrifice (Matthew 5:17).

Another prevalent Jewish belief of the period that fueled the fire of this controversy was the notion that salvation relied upon a treasury of good and bad works that an individual stored up for himself during the course of his lifetime. If a person had more good works than bad in his account, he was considered righteous and, therefore, saved. Furthermore, a person's store of good works could be supplemented by the surplus of good works performed by the patriarchs in his life in order to tip the scales in the individual's favor. Thus, in the minds of many Jews, salvation became a debt that God owed to man by virtue of the individual's goodness.[7]

THE LAW OF MOSES

This background information regarding the conditions and false beliefs peculiar to Paul's time sheds the additional light necessary to properly and fully understand his statement concerning "works." Clearly, Paul was faced with the challenge to convince the Jewish converts that they were not saved by the dead works of the Law of Moses. According to the orthodox Jews, the Law of Moses consists of 613 commandments as listed in the five books of Moses, a number which easily multiplies into the thousands when the Rabbinical rules of the Mishnah are included.[8]

In his popular work on the life of the Savior, Alfred Edersheim discussed in great length the burdensome legal restrictions imposed on the Jews by their religious leaders at the time of the founding of the ancient Christian Church. Consider the following example: "If on the Sabbath a wall had fallen on a person, and it were doubtful whether he was under the ruins or not, whether he was alive or dead, a Jew or Gentile, it would be duty to clear away the rubbish sufficiently to find the body. If life were not extinct, the labour would have to be continued; but if the person were dead nothing further should be done to extricate the body."

In another example of permissible Sabbath activity, Edersheim explains: "If a hen had laid on the Sabbath, the egg was forbidden, because, evidently, it could not have been destined on a weekday for eating, since it was not yet laid, and did not exist; while if the hen had been kept, not for laying but for fattening, the egg might be eaten as forming part of the hen that had fallen off!"[9] These are only two of thousands of similarly absurd restrictions which comprised the oppressive, meaningless system of worship devised by the degenerate Jewish leaders of this period. It is no wonder that Paul used such strong language to condemn the belief that this litany of legal restrictions was still in force for new converts of Christianity.

When people today read Paul's powerful arguments against the works of the Law of Moses, many wrongfully impose these same words on a modern Western society that is not characterized by this same zeal for excessive ritualistic detail. Thus, many modern-day believers tend to overreact or overcompensate in their interpretations of Paul's language by actually condemning all works, Mosaic or otherwise.

Paul's arguments were meant for Judaizers, or overzealous Jews who attempted to burden new Christian converts with corrupted Jewish law. They were not meant for modern readers who debate whether obedience to the Savior's teachings are essential to eternal life. For Paul, there would be no argument. He fervently taught that good works are necessary, but not the burdensome works of the Law of Moses. Those who deny that Paul preached the necessity of good works might be surprised to learn that in his New Testament letters he used the Greek word "ergon," which means "work" or "deed," over 80 times in conjunction with exhortations to the saints of the Church to do them.[10]

Paul also had to convince the people of his time that they were not the beneficiaries of salvation as payment owed to them by God due to their storehouse of good works. Salvation came exclusively by way of Christ's atoning sacrifice and obedience to His command-ments. While the dead works of the old law were rendered worthless in achieving man's eternal salvation, Paul nevertheless understood that Christ's gospel still required man's obedience and righteousness if he was to qualify for the redeeming power of the atonement. That is why he wrote in his epistle to the saints in Rome that God *"will render to every man according to his deeds:* To them who by patient *continuance in well doing* seek for glory and honour and immortality, *eternal life:* But unto them that are contentious and do not obey the truth, but obey unrighteousness, indignation and wrath" (Romans 2:6-8). Following Christ's crucifixion, man was relieved of his duty to perform the "works" of the Law of Moses, however he was in no way exempt from the "works" or obedience required by the eternal gospel of Jesus Christ.

GOSPEL WORKS VS. MOSAIC LAW WORKS

To further clarify this doctrinal issue, it is essential to point out the distinction between the "works" to which Paul often referred in many of his epistles to the early saints and the "works" to which Latter-day Saints give reference as being necessary to receive eternal salvation. They are not one and the same. Paul, when speaking of unnecessary works, was referring to the outward ordinances of the Law of Moses, such as animal sacrifice, dietary restrictions, and circumcision, as well as the thousands of corrupt Pharisaical legal requirements, whereas Latter-day Saints, when speaking of the works essential to salvation, are referring to obedience to the commandments and ordinances of the gospel of Jesus Christ.

Such commandments include the Ten Commandments (Exodus 20:3-17), high standards of sexual morality (Matthew 15:19-20; 1 Peter 2:11; 1 Corinthians 6:9-10), avoidance of alcoholic beverages and tobacco (Leviticus 10:9; Numbers 6:3; Proverbs 20:1; Isaiah 5:22; 1 Corinthians 3:16-17; 6:10; Ephesians 5:18), feeding the hungry and clothing the naked (Matthew 25:31-46), visiting the orphans and widows (James 1:27), loving one's neighbor (John 13:34-35), and so on. The gospel ordinances include baptism (Matthew 28:19; John 3:5; Mark 16:16; Luke 7:29-30; Acts 2:38), receiving the gift of the Holy Ghost (Acts 2:38; 8:14-21), and partaking of the sacrament (Matthew 26:26-27; John 6:54), to name a few. These God-ordained righteous activities, along with others, will serve as the basis for eternal judgment when the great Judge of all mankind, Jesus Christ, shall return to "reward every man according to his works" (Matthew 16:27).

The Law of Moses was given to the Israelites as a lesser law to prepare them for the fullness of the gospel. As Paul stated, "The law was our schoolmaster to bring us unto Christ, that we might be justified by faith" (Galatians 3:24). All things performed in the Mosaic Law, such as animal sacrifice, were done to turn the hearts and minds of the participants towards the impending atonement of the coming Messiah, Jesus Christ. The Law of Moses was a set of outward performances or carnal commandments "which stood in meats and drinks, and diverse washings, and carnal ordinances, imposed on them until the time of reformation [the first coming of Jesus Christ]" (Hebrews 9:10). (For greater detail of the requirements of the Law of Moses refer to the books of Exodus, Leviticus, Numbers, and Deuteronomy).

The Israelites were given this lesser law "because of transgression" (Galatians 3:19), meaning they were not yet spiritually prepared to live the higher law of the gospel of Jesus Christ. As a preparatory law, or "schoolmaster" as Paul put it, the Law of Moses "could not make him that did the service perfect" (Hebrews 9:9). Only faith in the Savior and obedience to His higher law, the eternal gospel, can effectuate eternal salvation. It was for this reason that Paul said that man cannot be saved by works, meaning the works of the Law of Moses. He was not referring to good Christian works of righteousness, nor was he speaking of obedience to the Savior's commandments.

THE LAW OF CHRIST

In his letter to the Galatians, Paul admonished the saints to "bear ye one another's burdens," for this was the essence of "the law of Christ" (Galatians 6:2). While the Law of Moses taught the principle of an "eye for eye, tooth for tooth" (Exodus 21:24), the higher Law of Christ required the Lord's disciples to love one another, even one's enemies. Love is the central theme and purpose of all God's commandments; they teach us to love God, our fellowman, and the ways of righteousness.

By way of Christ's atoning sacrifice, the lesser law, the Law of Moses, was fulfilled, and thereby replaced by the higher law of the gospel of Jesus Christ. To illustrate this point, the Savior declared, "Ye have heard that it was said by them of old time, Thou shalt not kill; and whosoever shall kill shall be in danger of the judgment: But I say unto you, That whosoever is angry with his brother without a cause shall be in danger of the judgment: and whosoever shall say to his brother, Raca [word suggesting contempt], shall be in danger of the council: but whosoever shall say, Thou fool, shall be in danger of hell fire" (Matthew 5:21-22). He also taught, "Ye have heard that it was said by them of old time, Thou shalt not commit adultery: But I say unto you, that whosoever looketh on a woman to lust after her hath committed adultery with her already in his heart" (Matthew 5:27-28).

A complete reading of the Sermon on the Mount will reveal the fact that Christ did not abolish the law nor the need to obey His commandments. Christ gave a higher law and greater commandments. Even though His redeeming sacrifice rendered such carnal ordinances as animal sacrifice and circumcision unnecessary and obsolete, His eternal commandments are as binding upon us today as they were upon people of earlier times.

Who would dare have us believe that Christ's atonement eliminates the need to refrain from acts of murder, adultery, thievery, or the like? Or who would attempt to convince us that the atonement relieves us of our duty to love our neighbor and assist the poor, sick, and afflicted? Most importantly, who would have us believe that it is permissable to place other gods before our Father in Heaven, to worship graven images and idols, or to take the name of the Lord our God in vain?

In His parable of the sheep and the goats, the Savior sought to impress upon His disciples the importance of caring for the less fortunate members of society. He drew the minds of His audience to the day when He would stand in final judgment of the world. At the time of His Second Coming, Jesus Christ shall sit upon His throne of glory to judge all mankind, and "before him shall be gathered all nations: and he shall separate them one from another, as a shepherd divideth his sheep from the goats: and he shall set the sheep on his right hand, but the goats on the left" (Matthew 25:31-33).

The Lord then explained that those found on His right will inherit eternal life, for they represent His obedient followers who fed the hungry, gave drink to the thirsty, clothed the naked, and visited the sick and the prisoners (Matthew 25:34-40). "For I was an hungered, and ye gave me meat: I was thirsty, and ye gave me drink: I was a stranger, and ye took me in: Naked, and ye clothed me: I was sick, and ye visited me: I was in prison, and ye came unto me" (Matthew 25:35-36). In other words, those who stand at His right hand, the "blessed of [the] Father", demonstrated their love for God and man by performing acts of kindness and charity for the destitute and downtrodden. The Savior declared, "Inasmuch as ye have done it unto one of the least of these my brethren, ye have done it unto me" (Matthew 25:40).

As for those on the Lord's left, they represent those who failed to serve their God in neglecting the hungry, naked, and sick (Matthew 25:41-44). They are cast from His presence for their disobedience to God and lack of charity toward their fellow man. "For I was an hungered, and ye gave me no meat: I was thirsty, and ye gave me no drink: I was a stranger, and ye took me not in: naked, and ye clothed me not: sick, and in prison, and ye visited me not" (Matthew 25:42-43).

The Lord severely chastises these spiritual goats: "Verily I say unto you, Inasmuch as ye did it not to one of the least of these, ye did it not to me. And these shall go away into everlasting punishment: but the righteous into life eternal" (Matthew 25:45-46).

The message of this parable is clear. Those of God's children who exercise Christ-like charity toward their fellow beings will be worthy of eternal life. The Savior will say to them, "Come, ye blessed of my Father, inherit the kingdom prepared for you from the foundation of the world" (Matthew 25:34). Those who do not care for the needy will be "cursed, into everlasting fire, prepared for the devil and his angels" (Matthew 25:41). The eternal salvation of man requires much more than belief; it demands Christian works of love, righteousness, and obedience as revealed in this powerful parable told by the Savior.

At the conclusion of his great Sermon on the Mount, the Savior taught, again speaking in parables, that he who hears His teachings and *does them* is likened unto a wise man who will not fall during times of trial and adversity. However, he that hears His teachings and *does them not* is likened unto a foolish man and great will be his fall (Matthew 7:24-27). And great will be our fall if we do not obey God's commandments.

JUSTIFIED BY THE WORKS OF THE GOSPEL

Paul wrote another passage that is frequently misunderstood in his epistle to the saints at Galatia, "But that no man is justified by the law in the sight of God, it is evident: for, the just shall live by faith" (Galatians 3:11). In this case, as in almost all cases where the word "law" is used by Paul, he is referring to the Law of Moses and not the higher "law of Christ" (Galatians 6:2). He preached emphatically that man "could not be justified by the law of Moses" (Acts 13:39); salvation did not come by performing the works of this obsolete law. Nevertheless, Paul was aware of the necessity of living Christ's higher gospel law, having taught the saints in Rome that "the hearers of the law are not just before God, but the *doers of the law shall be justified*" (Romans 2:13). In this scripture, Paul is referring to the Law of Christ, that is, the fullness of the gospel. James also had Christ's higher law in mind when he wrote, "Ye see then how that *by works a man is justified, and not by faith only*" (James 2:24).

Latter-day Saints indeed realize that salvation does not come by way of the works of the Law of Moses nor by virtue of a storehouse of good works, yet they do believe that the good works of righteous Christian living and obedience to God's commandments does qualify them for the cleansing power of Christ's redeeming blood. While it is true that the blessings of God are not in any way earned by man, it is also true that "when we obtain any blessing from God, it is by obedience to that law upon which it is predicated" (Doctrine & Covenants 130:20). If we want a healthy body, we must observe correct principles of diet, exercise, and rest. If we want to obtain knowledge, we must be willing to pay the price in terms of diligent study and practical experience. If we seek eternal life, then we must understand that the requirements for salvation established by the Lord are satisfied through faith and obedience. God does give freely, but only to those who seek to observe His divine will.

Perhaps an analogy will best illustrate the LDS Church's stand on the relationship between faith and works. A farmer cannot expect to harvest a crop come harvest time if he neglects to sow any seed. Likewise, he must till the ground, fertilize the soil, irrigate the land, and harvest the crop, among other chores. After these tasks are completed, is the farmer then entitled to receive all the credit for his bounteous crop? Who provided the fertile soil, the germ of life in the seeds, the sun's life-giving rays, and the rain which nourishes his crops?

Indeed, if not for the grace of God, the farmer would have no crop to harvest, yet God's grace does not render the farmer's efforts unnecessary. Both the grace of God and the efforts of the farmer were required to produce a successful crop.[11] Likewise, Latter-day Saints believe that both the grace of God and our individual efforts are necessary ingredients in our quest for eternal life.

As previously discussed, the grace of God consists of all those things which the Almighty has done to bring to pass our eternal salvation that we are incapable of performing for ourselves. This suggests that not only are there certain things that we are able to do to improve our own chances for salvation, but there are things which God expects us to do.

Man is not totally powerless to act; as a gift from God, he has been granted his free will. God has created man as a thinking, acting, sentient being, capable of choosing between good and evil, virtue and vice, light and darkness. While man may be powerless to bring about his own salvation, he possesses the freedom and ability to think and act for himself. He has the power to repent of his sinful behavior and obey the commandments of God. This is exactly what God requires of His children in order to qualify for His grace and receive the blessings of eternal life.

What good and righteous parent, who wants his children to learn, grow, develop character, and assume responsibility, would tell his children to take no active part in their own personal progression or improvement? Imagine telling your children, "Sit down and relax. Don't bother doing anything for yourself. I'll do everything for you because I love you. Don't waste your time working, studying, or serving others. Nothing you can do will prove useful to your personal development. Simply believe that I will do everything for you and all will be well with you."

Any prudent parent realizes that this is a prescription for failure. A truly loving parent would instruct his or her children to take responsibility for their own lives and actions, teach them the value of hard work, challenge them by setting high, yet attainable, goals and standards, and reward them according to their obedience as tempered by their abilities and opportunities. A parent who offers everything for nothing ends up with a child who knows little about anything. Surely our Heavenly Father knows better than even the wisest of earthly parents how to raise the best children possible, which is why His faithful servant, the Apostle Paul, never taught, "Do nothing for your salvation." Rather, he instructed true followers of Christ to "work out your own salvation" (Philippians 2:12), implying that we each play a crucial and active role in this process of qualifying for the blessings of Jesus Christ's atonement.

As part of their spiritual growth and development, God expects His children to do all they are capable of doing for themselves. This in no way diminishes the power of the atonement of Christ, yet the Savior has made it clear that He will redeem only those that endeavor with all their might to overcome their personal sins through the process of sincere repentance and righteous behavior, making Him the "author of eternal salvation unto all them that obey him" (Hebrews 5:9). As we strive to obey God's will, "through the blood of the everlasting covenant" Jesus Christ can "make [us] perfect in every good work" (Hebrews 13:20-21).

The Lord's eternal kingdom is a holy and righteous place where His children are granted special privileges and powers. Only those that have faith in Christ and demonstrate that they are willing and able to live by heavenly standards of righteousness will prove worthy to be cleansed by the Savior's blood, thereby gaining entrance to our Heavenly Father's kingdom.

Latter-day Saints believe the saving power of Christ's atonement is infinite and eternal; it is our own disobedience to the will of the Father that limits our spiritual progression and jeopardizes our eternal salvation. If we have done all that we possibly can, like the wise and diligent farmer seeking a bounteous harvest, and have humbled ourselves before God, the Lord will extend the redeeming power and grace of His atoning sacrifice to us and do all that is necessary to assure our salvation from spiritual death and personal sin. "Be not deceived; God is not mocked: for whatsoever a man soweth, that shall he also reap" (Galatians 6:7).

THE FRUITS OF LIP SERVICE

A brief glance at today's newspaper headlines along with recent statistics monitoring crime, the U.S. economy, and American educational achievements, will reveal a most alarming trend. These facts and figures portend a bleak outlook for the American cultural and economic landscape.

Are we witnessing the decline and fall of American civilization within our own lifetime? What is causing the moral deterioration of the most prosperous nation ever to grace the earth? Why is the most vibrant and productive economy man has ever known beginning to show cracks in its financial structure, showing signs of imminent collapse? Why are we witnessing increased incidences of murder, rape, drug abuse, robbery, theft, adultery, premarital promiscuity, homosexuality, child and spouse abuse, and abortion, as well as a worsening of economic indicators such as our foreign trade imbalance, poverty level, unemployment rate, capital spending, inflation, and personal, corporate, and government debt? To borrow the Apostle Paul's terminology, are Americans reaping what they sow?

According to recent polls, America is overwhelmingly a Christian nation. A recent study, conducted by two professors at the City University of New York, in which 113,000 American adults participated, disclosed that 90 percent of Americans identify themselves as religious.[12] Another survey conducted by the ICR Survey Research Group of Media, Pennsylvania, determined that 86 percent of Americans identify themselves as Christians.[13] How could a nation wherein 86 of every 100 citizens profess themselves to be disciples of Christ be headed for temporal and spiritual disaster? How could this great Christian nation possibly incur the anger of the same Lord they claim to worship and honor? Surely, if 86% of Americans are Christians, it can't be a lack of "belief." What are Americans doing wrong?

Another more comprehensive survey recently published in book form perhaps offers some answers. According to this nation-wide study, which promised complete anonymity to its participants in order to acquire honest responses, 90 percent of the respondents claimed they truly believe in God.[14] The participants also admitted to some less flattering details regarding their personal attitudes and beliefs.

The survey results revealed that 77 percent of Americans do not see the point in observing the Sabbath, 74 percent will steal from those who won't miss it, 91 percent lie on a regular basis, 53 percent will cheat on their spouse, 30 percent will cheat on their taxes, 50 percent will put in less than an honest day's work, and 41 percent use recreational drugs. From the victim's perspective, 20 percent admit they have been date-raped. These figures are a serious indictment against the American people, for clearly they have rejected the commandments of God.

The survey further reveals that only 11 percent of Americans believe in observing all Ten Commandments.[15] A mere 17 percent of all Americans consider it a sin to go against God's will.[16] It is no wonder the moral fabric of American society is deteriorating.

Are society's woes and its almost universal rejection of the commandments of God a direct reflection or result of the modern-day doctrine that man is saved by grace alone, regardless of his deeds? What motivation is there to observe God's commandments if salvation can be achieved without obedience? When those in Christendom are led to believe that God will save them in their sins, they see no need to repent and obey. The commandments of God become nothing more than quaint suggestions when they are separated from their intended consequences, namely, eternal rewards for obedience and eternal punishment for disobedience. As we search for parallels between ancient scriptural history and modern times, it becomes increasingly clear that Americans are reaping the bitter harvest of their beliefs, as well as their unrighteous practices.

According to the same poll, 46 percent of Americans expect to spend eternity in heaven, while only 4 percent anticipate a future existence in hell.[17] Apparently, many Americans are either not familiar with or choose to ignore the teachings of Christ's early apostles on this matter.

In one of his letters to the Corinthians, Paul taught, "Be not deceived: neither fornicators...nor adulterers...shall inherit the kingdom of God" (1 Corinthians 6:9-10), however at least 45 percent of those Americans professing to be Christians admit that they have or will commit adultery if given the chance. The Apostle John taught that "all liars shall have their part in the lake which burneth with fire and brimstone: which is the second death" (Revelation 21:8), yet 91 percent of Americans and at least 90 percent of Christian Americans admit to lying on a regular basis.

The ancient American prophet, Nephi, foresaw the widespread acceptance of this false teaching of salvation by grace alone in our day: "And there shall also be many which shall say: Eat, drink, and be merry: nevertheless, fear God — he will justify in committing a little sin; yea, lie a little, take the advantage of one because of his words, dig a pit for thy neighbor; there is no harm in this; and do all these things, for tomorrow we die; and if it so be that we are guilty, God will beat us with a few stripes, and at last we shall be saved in the kingdom of God.

"Yea, and there shall be many which shall teach after this manner, false and vain and foolish doctrines, and shall be puffed up in their hearts, and shall seek deep to hide their counsels from the Lord; and their works shall be in the dark" (The Book of Mormon, 2 Nephi 28:8-9).

Throughout the ages, the Lord has plainly conveyed His intentions to bless His children with temporal and spiritual prosperity when they observe His commandments, and likewise withhold His blessings from the disobedient. In the Old Testament, the Lord informed the ancient Israelites, "If ye walk in my statutes, and keep my commandments, and do them; Then I will give you rain in due season, and the land shall yield her increase, and the trees of the field shall yield their fruit" (Leviticus 26:3-4). The Lord then enumerates the many other blessings awaiting those who will but keep His commandments (Leviticus 26:5-13). On the other hand, He discloses in great detail the punishments in store for those who choose the path of disobedience: "But if ye will not hearken unto me, and will not do all these commandments; And if ye shall despise my statutes, or if your soul abhor my judgments, so that ye will not do all my commandments, but that ye break my covenant: I also will do this unto you; I will even appoint over you terror, consumption, and the burning ague, that shall consume the eyes, and cause sorrow of heart: and ye shall sow your seed in vain, for your enemies shall eat it" (Leviticus 26:14-16). The Lord then describes in detail many other cursings to be visited upon his disobedient children (Leviticus 26:17-39; see also Deuteronomy 6).

In the Book of Mormon, the Lord has declared, through His ancient American prophet Lehi, the following revelation concerning this great American continent: "Wherefore, I, Lehi, prophesy according to the workings of the Spirit which is in me, that there shall none come into this land save they shall be brought by the hand of the Lord.

"Wherefore, this land is consecrated unto him whom he shall bring. And if it so be that they shall serve him according to the commandments which he hath given, it shall be a land of liberty unto them; wherefore, they shall never be brought down into captivity; if so, it shall be because of iniquity; for if iniquity shall abound cursed shall be the land for their sakes, but unto the righteous it shall be blessed forever...

"And he hath said that: Inasmuch as ye shall keep my commandments ye shall prosper in the land; but inasmuch as ye will not keep my commandments ye shall be cut off from my presence" (The Book of Mormon, 2 Nephi 1:6-7,20).

This divine promise applies as much to modern Americans as it did to our ancient American forerunners. We will receive untold earthly blessings as well as eternal life when we obey God's word, however we will incur His wrath and forfeit these blessings, including eternal life, if we fail to heed His commands. The truthfulness of this doctrine is becoming more and more evident with each passing year.

SAVED BY GRACE — EXALTED BY GRACE AND WORKS

Latter-day Saints do believe that man is saved by grace, for were it not for the atonement of Jesus Christ all of an individual's good works and righteous deeds would be of no worth to he that performed them. Man is powerless to save himself, which is why an ancient American prophet wrote, "It is by grace that we are saved, *after all we can do"* (The Book of Mormon, 2 Nephi 25:23). In other words, even after we repent of our sins and obey God's commandments, it is still God's grace that saves us from death and sin, lifting us from our lowly state to an exalted station in His holy kingdom. Through obedience and righteousness, we have merely met the Savior's requirements to receive His grace, thus rendering ourselves eligible for His atoning and exalting power.

The Lord extends His grace to the obedient, for "the Lord will *give grace* and glory: no good thing will be withhold from them that *walk uprightly"* (Psalms 84:11), that is, from them that obey His commandments (Deut. 8:6). The Apostle James wrote that the Lord "giveth grace unto the humble" (James 4:6), the humble being those that submit to God's will. God will not extend His exalting grace to those who fail to repent and obey, regardless of any self-acclaimed "belief" in Jesus Christ. Only after we have demonstrated our love for and faith in God by forsaking unrighteousness, does God's grace become operative in our lives, sanctifying us of all ungodliness, and consequently, Christ becomes "the author of eternal salvation unto all them that *obey* him" (Hebrews 5:9). In essence, we are saved by the grace of God unto eternal life after we have manifested our faith in and love for Him with our good Christian works of righteousness.

In a letter to Titus, the Apostle Paul explained that their quest for righteous obedience would set Christ's true disciples apart from the rest of the world: "For the grace of God that bringeth salvation hath appeared to all men, teaching us that, denying ungodliness and worldly lusts, we should live soberly, righteously, and godly, in this present world; looking for that blessed hope, and the glorious appearing of the great God and our Saviour Jesus Christ; Who gave himself for us, that he might redeem us from all iniquity, and purify unto himself *a peculiar people, zealous of good works"* (Titus 2:11-14).

Just as the Bible teaches the necessity of obedience to God, its companion scripture, the Book of Mormon, also conveys this eternal principle of salvation. After His resurrection, the Savior appeared to His disciples in the ancient American continents to provide witness of His atoning sacrifice and give divine instruction. Among the many glorious teachings He imparted, He shared the following words concerning the Law of Moses and His eternal gospel: "Think not that I am come to destroy the law or the prophets. I am not come to destroy but to fulfil;

"For verily I say unto you, one jot nor one tittle hath not passed away from the law, but in me it hath all been fulfilled.

"And behold, I have given you the law and the commandments of my Father, that ye shall believe in me, and that ye shall repent of your sins, and come unto me with a broken heart and a contrite spirit. Behold, ye have the commandments before you, and the law is fulfilled.

"Therefore come unto me and be ye saved; for verily I say unto you, that except ye shall keep my commandments, which I have commanded you at this time, ye shall in no case enter into the kingdom of heaven" (The Book of Mormon, 3 Nephi 12:17-20). The Savior taught his disciples that observance of the Law of Moses was no longer necessary, having been fulfilled in His atoning sacrifice, however He emphasized the importance of keeping His eternal commandments.

Hear the powerful words of the Lord in these latter days, as they decisively lay to rest any confusion or debate on this matter: "Verily, thus saith the Lord: It shall come to pass that every soul who forsaketh his sins and cometh unto me, and calleth on my name, and obeyeth my voice, and keepeth my commandments, shall see my face and know that I am" (D&C 93:1).

"And all that call upon the name of the Lord, and keep his commandments, shall be saved. Even so. Amen" (D&C 100:17).

"If you keep not my commandments you cannot be saved in the kingdom of my Father. Behold, I, Jesus Christ, your Lord and your God, and your Redeemer, by the power of my Spirit have spoken it. Amen" (D&C 18:46-47).

While on the island of Patmos, the Apostle John received a glorious revelation, which came to be known as just that — The Revelation. Among many other glorious visions, he was treated to a brief glimpse of God's celestial kingdom. Likening heaven unto a great city and eternal life unto a tree, John wrote, "Blessed are they that *do his commandments*, that they may have right to the tree of life, and may enter in through the gates into the city" (Revelation 22:14). May each one of us partake of the tree of eternal life and enter into God's glorious kingdom by exercising faith in our Savior, Jesus Christ, and obeying His commandments.

5

DIVINE REVELATION

THE Lord's Church is organized in a manner that allows its members regular opportunities to hear the words of the Lord's appointed servants in order to receive enlightenment and training. One such occasion occurred while I was still living in Fresno, California, a member of barely a few years. All the local priesthood leaders in central California were invited to attend a Regional Priesthood Leadership Meeting, over which President Howard W. Hunter, the president of the Quorum of the Twelve Apostles, would preside. He was joined by Elder Dallin H. Oaks, a member of the Quorum of the Twelve Apostles; Elder John Carmack, another general authority of the Church; as well as approximately one thousand local members of the Church.

A friend and I arrived at the meeting just as the opening hymn was being sung, only to find that the chapel and cultural hall were packed. We were soon informed by an usher that there were a few available seats in the front row. People typically avoid the front row for various reasons, such as the angle of view due to close proximity to the speaker's podium. With few other options, we decided that it would be exciting to sit that close to two apostles of the Lord. For someone who wanted to remain inconspicuous, that would turn out to be my first mistake.

As the four-hour meeting progressed, it proved to be a veritable feast of practical and spiritual insights. Less than an hour into the proceedings, President Hunter took the stand and favored all those present with his experience and wisdom. He chose as his topic the true meaning of the term "gospel," and as his text he chose the 27th chapter of Third Nephi in the Book of Mormon which powerfully defines the gospel of Jesus Christ. As he stood at the podium, he began to open his scriptures, then looked around the full hall until his eyes rested directly upon me.

He said, "Young man, would you be kind enough to come up and read for me?"

Fear struck my heart. I thought to myself, "Is he talking to me?"

"Yes, young man, you. Please come up."

There have been very few times in my life when I have been stricken with fear — this was one of those times. The walk to the stand seemed like an incredible journey, yet I finally made it, standing before a thousand of my amused peers, not to mention about three feet away from the President of the Quorum of the Twelve Apostles. As I stood next to him at the stand, he put his arm around me and pulled me in close, thus making sure that I couldn't get away. There we stood with our arms around each other like two young school mates, my knees shaking and his knees as solid as a rock. It was obvious which of us had done this before.

He asked my name then said, "Brother Brase, please start reading right here, and I'll tell you when to stop." He pointed to the page, and I began to read from the Book of Third Nephi with some fear and trembling. After what seemed like an eternity, he finally said, "Stop, please." I thought I had read nearly the entire page, yet my mental state precluded me from assimilating anything I had just read.

President Hunter continued, "Let me explain what these scriptures mean." He proceeded to exhibit the spirit and authority of his sacred calling as an apostle of Jesus Christ by beautifully opening the scriptures to our eyes and ears. The Spirit of God bore witness to me that this was a true apostle of the Lord Jesus Christ, having been called of God by direct revelation. What a privilege it was to hear his inspiring commentary on the scriptures.

After five minutes of scriptural interpretation, he looked over to me and said, "Please continue reading, Brother Brase." I did as he asked, reading what seemed to have been another entire page of scripture before he again quietly said, "Stop."

I then expected him to expound further on the scriptures, but instead he turned to me and asked, "Now, Brother Brase, what does this scripture mean?" Fear turned to terror as my mind went blank. I thought to myself, "I have no idea what I just read, and there isn't time now to read it again. What am I going to say? These brethren are expecting a response now." I'm sure the panic was discernible for everyone to see, as incoherent thoughts raced through my mind. By now a low murmur of subdued chuckles could be heard spreading through the chapel, as my fellow brethren pondered — more likely enjoyed — my predicament and anticipated my response. I thought they all seemed awfully cool and calm considering my dilemma. The President of the Quorum of the Twelve Apostles had just asked me to interpret a full page of scripture for him and one thousand other priesthood leaders, and I had no idea what I had just read.

As I stared blankly at the open book before me, again I pondered President Hunter's question, "What does this scripture mean?" Finally, I glanced over at him with a helpless look and replied, almost inaudibly, "Don't you know?" To this day, I still can't believe I said it. It was as though somebody else spoke the words while I moved my lips. I truly felt like someone's dummy, however, this slip of the tongue proved to be an answer to my unspoken prayer. The entire congregation broke into thunderous laughter which seemed to go on for minutes. When I saw President Hunter and Elders Oaks and Carmack likewise enjoying this jovial moment, I knew that I just might live to tell this story to my grandchildren.

When the laughter finally died down, President Hunter again put his arm around me and exclaimed, "I can see I chose the right man for the job." He then asked me to continue reading several more verses of scripture before graciously allowing me to return to the refuge of my seat. Perhaps he felt that anyone who could come up with such an unexpected response deserved to be released from his awful fate.

Despite my nerve-wracking experience, I was thankful for the witness I had received that this was a servant of God and that he had been sent by a living prophet to teach and expound to us the true gospel of Jesus Christ. To sit at the feet — or to stand shoulder-to-shoulder — with one of Christ's chosen servants as he opened the scriptures to our understanding through the instrumentality of the Holy Ghost, was indeed a faith promoting experience. I knew then, as I know now, that President Hunter spoke with all of the authority of the Apostle Paul or any of the other ancient apostles. Once again, the Lord has established His church on the bedrock of continuous revelation.

As Latter-day Saints, "we believe all that God has revealed, all that he does now reveal, and we believe that he will yet reveal many great and important things pertaining to the Kingdom of God" (Ninth Article of Faith). We believe the heavens are open and that God continues to make His will known to man through living prophets and apostles. Latter-day Saints do not subscribe to the popular teaching that the heavens are closed and that revelation is finished. We do not believe that the need for prophets or revelation has passed simply because we have a portion of the revelations of ancient prophets. Rather, we believe that God continues to talk to His children just as He did anciently. We testify to the world that He has given more revelation and scripture for the benefit of man in these last days.

Continuous Revelation

Latter-day Saints believe that God deals with His children "the same yesterday, and today, and forever" (Hebrews 13:8), and if He loved His children enough anciently to give them prophets who could receive direct revelation that would bless the lives of men, then He would do so again today. If He did not, then He would be an unjust God, favoring one generation over another. Yet, God does love the children of this generation as much as He has loved those of any other generation, for all people of all dispensations of time are His children. He is a just and loving Father. For this reason He has blessed us with prophets and apostles who are contemporary with our day in order that we might know His will regarding the manner in which we should conduct our daily lives and prepare ourselves for future events. We invite all people of all nations to witness for themselves the glorious gospel truths which have been restored to the earth through the prophets of these latter days.

Even though the ancient scriptures contain many eternal truths that have much application in our lives today, they also contain much that is specific instruction for those of another time, such as the requirements of the Law of Moses as revealed in the Pentateuch (first five books of the Old Testament). Our present-day society is different in many ways from any other that has preceded it. We are confronted by many trials and challenges that are unique to our time. If not for continuing revelation, we might not know how, as Christians, to deal with certain situations that have never before arisen in the history of mankind.

Imagine what might have happened if Noah had not received divine instruction to build an ark, but instead depended solely on previously received revelations to determine his course of action (Genesis 6). What would have been the consequences if Moses was not called by God through the avenue of direct revelation to lead Israel out of Egypt and across the Red Sea to the promised land, but instead was forced to rely solely on the scriptures to learn God's will on this matter (Exodus 3)? Likewise, if not for continuing revelation, Peter would not have received the command in a vision to take the gospel message to all nations and peoples, that is, to the Gentiles as well as the Jews (Acts 10).

These servants of God did not depend on past revelations or existing scriptural writings to determine their respective God-given duties in order to deal with the circumstances at hand. Noah did not depend on Adam's revelations to build his ark, Moses did not rely on Noah's revelations to lead Israel out of bondage, nor did Peter require Moses' revelations to spread the Savior's gospel to the Gentiles.[1] Each received direct revelation, current to their time, in order to fulfill God's designs and make His immediate will known to their fellowman.

With today's trials and temptations and the impending events of future days, such as the War of Armageddon and the Second Coming of Jesus Christ, surely there are divine instructions we have yet to receive in order that we might prepare ourselves for these and other unique circumstances to come. Revelations received by Noah or Moses regarding their temporal instructions will be of little value when it comes to our own temporal preparations for the future.

Suppose the Lord wanted His disciples to assemble somewhere or do something in particular in order to prepare for some future event such as He required of the ancient Israelites. Who would receive such revelations? There must be a living prophet, for "surely the Lord God will do nothing, but he revealeth his secret unto his servants the prophets" (Amos 3:7).

Latter-day Saints believe that God's most current word is the most binding on His children. When the Savior came to earth to preach His Father's gospel, His latest instructions on how to live and worship rendered the Law of Moses obsolete. The preparatory Mosaic Law had been fulfilled in Christ's atoning sacrifice and a higher gospel law was introduced. This transition demonstrates that a commandment issued by the Lord yesterday can be revoked today, just as a commandment given today can be repealed tomorrow. The Almighty Lord always maintains this prerogative.

The most dramatic chapter in the life of Abraham possibly best illustrates this principle of continuing revelation. When the Lord commanded Abraham to slay his son, Isaac, this latest divine instruction overruled an earlier commandment which made the act of killing another person a grievous sin (Genesis 9:6). As Abraham was about to carry out the Lord's wishes, an angel of the Lord said, "Lay not thine hand upon the lad" (Genesis 22:12). Again the Lord changed His command to Abraham. Abraham was under obligation to observe the first commandment until he received the second, then he was under obligation to perform the third commandment instead of the second.

The latest instruction from the Lord always remains the most binding until further instruction is given. God's work is progressive. While eternal truths never change, the means, methods, and procedures for fulfilling God's plans are subject to His immediate will.[2] Without a prophet to receive His most current divine directives, we are lost.

The Bible teaches us that God's children throughout the ages were never expected to deal with life's challenges solely by means of past revelation or instruction intended for another time, people, or circumstance. God has always been gracious enough to bless His children that seek to know His will with the knowledge requisite to their spiritual and temporal survival. Despite the fact that those who lived anciently possessed scriptures of their own, received by prophets long past, and despite their ability to communicate with God through prayer as facilitated by the Holy Ghost, the Lord also granted them divine guidance via holy prophets, endowing them with knowledge of God's immediate will.

ORTHODOXY

In every historical dispensation, it has been difficult for God's children to accept living prophets. When Noah warned the people of their iniquity prior to the Flood, only seven others beside himself heeded his words. When Christ preached the gospel of salvation during His mortal ministry, total conversion to His teachings was the exception and not the rule.

And so it is today. God again has spoken to us through living, modern-day prophets and apostles. At the head of The Church of Jesus Christ of Latter-day Saints is a true and living prophet of God, as well as twelve apostles of the Lord Jesus Christ. As in the past, these men are unfortunately regarded as God's appointed messengers by only a very small portion of our Heavenly Father's children.

The recorded history of mankind reveals that the truth has never been popular. The Old Testament is replete with examples of God's children worshipping false gods and handmade idols while the teachings of the prophets fell upon deaf ears. The Lord, in His compassion toward His children, "sent to them messengers" to teach them true doctrine, yet "they mocked the messengers of God, and despised his words, and misused his prophets" (2 Chronicles 36:15-16). So universal was the rejection of God's word that Stephen asked the question of his angry assailants at the time of his stoning, "Which of the prophets have not your fathers persecuted?" (Acts 7:52).

Orthodoxy, that is, practices and beliefs conforming to the established or conventional religious doctrine of the day, has never represented the Lord's true gospel — not in Noah's day, not in Christ's day, not in our day. The apostles of the first-century Church preached doctrines that were considered heretical by the orthodox religious community of their day. The high priest Ananias and an orator named Tertullus accused the Apostle Paul of being "a pestilent fellow, and a mover of sedition among all the Jews throughout the world, and a ringleader of the sect of the Nazarenes" (Acts 24:5).

Paul's experiences show that the beliefs of the early saints were no more popular in his day than are the beliefs of the saints today. In Rome, Paul petitioned an audience of the Jewish religious leaders to appeal his case before them and expound the teachings of the gospel of Jesus Christ. The Jewish leaders responded, "We desire to hear of thee what thou thinkest: for as concerning this sect [of the Nazarenes], we know that *everywhere it is spoken against*" (Acts 28:22).

Gross misunderstanding and religious persecution have always been associated with those bearing the truth. This religious ostracism is one of the signs of the true Church. If history and the scriptures have taught us anything on this matter, it is this: spiritual truths are rarely popular with the people at large.

LIVING PROPHETS

Many people today find it relatively easy to believe that prophets walked the earth anciently, but to suggest that prophets live today readily invites skepticism or doubt. Perhaps it is too close to home, "for Jesus himself testified, that a prophet hath no honour in his own country" (John 4:44). People of ancient cultures claimed to have believed in the prophets of an even earlier day while rejecting their contemporaries (Matthew 23:29-32). Little has changed, for many today profess to believe in the Old and New Testament prophets while ignoring those of our day.

It is always easier to believe in dead prophets than those who are living, since their teachings can be easily manipulated to conform to an individual's preconceived beliefs or present lifestyle. Dead prophets are not available to offer correct interpretations of their writings or defend their teachings, whereas the words of living prophets offer less flexibility by virtue of their clarity of language and proximity in time.

In quoting the words of an early Christian martyr, one might ask, "Why should the present have less authority than the past because of some superstitious veneration of mere antiquity?"[3] Most people would have little trouble accepting a story of a man who walked and talked with God 2,000 or more years ago, but would hesitate to accept the idea of such a thing occurring today. What scriptural basis do they offer to support such a position? Where do the scriptures declare that the heavens are closed and that revelation is dead? Are we to believe that there is no need for prophets today, while five billion of God's children are on earth being "tossed to and fro, and carried about with every wind of doctrine" (Ephesians 4:14), and while wickedness and ungodliness are confronting them at every turn?

If God called prophets anciently, why would He not call them today? Does He love us any less than He loved those who lived before? Do we have less need of God today? Has God lost His power or will to communicate with His children? Is not Jesus Christ "the same yesterday, and today, and forever" (Hebrews 13:8)? Latter-day Saints believe that the love of God extends to all those who have lived, who presently live, and who will live on the earth in the future. For this reason, He has sent us prophets as He did in times past in order to reveal His will to those that seek it.

FOUNDATION OF APOSTLES AND PROPHETS

The Latter-day Saints believe that Christ's Church is founded on the principle of continuing revelation from God as conveyed to living prophets and apostles. The Bible supports the idea that prophets and apostles are essential to the existence and proper functioning of the Church. In his letter to the saints at Ephesus, Paul likened the Church to a house or building: "Now therefore ye are no more strangers and foreigners, but fellow citizens with the saints, and of the household of God; And are built upon the *foundation of the apostles and prophets*, Jesus Christ himself being the chief corner stone" (Ephesians 2:19-20). Just as a house without a solid foundation would collapse, so, too, would the Church without a foundation of apostles and prophets. The spiritual decline of the early Church following the death of Christ's apostles confirms this point.

Today, many teach that we no longer need apostles and prophets to guide us, thereby promoting the idea that the ancient apostles merely built the foundation of the Church, leaving the construction of the remainder of this allegorical structure to the modern Church membership at large. The assertion is made that modern-day believers must finish what the ancient apostles started; we must erect the supporting walls on their initiatory work and put the protective roof in place.

Paul employed an analogy in his letter to the Ephesians that sheds some light on this topic. He likened the members of the Church to a building. The living apostles and prophets who guided the Church via continuous revelation from God did not build the foundation — they were the foundation. In his epistle, Paul wrote that they, as church members, were "built upon the foundation of apostles and prophets," not that the foundation was built by the apostles and prophets (Ephesians 2:19-20). In this analogy, the other members of the Church were not the builders of the remaining edifice — they were the edifice. If the foundation of living apostles is removed, as by death, the structure will fall, for there is nothing on which the remaining members can be built. With the loss of the apostles, the Church lost its foundation of revelation and spiritual leadership, resulting in apostasy.

In his letter to the Corinthians, Paul drew upon another analogy between the Church and the human body: "For as the body is one, and hath many members, and all the members of that one body, being many, are one body: so also is Christ. For by one Spirit are we all baptized into one body" (1 Corinthians 12:12-13). Using this insightful analogy, Paul goes on to explain that each part of the body is necessary for the proper functioning of the entire organism, just as each member is essential to the proper functioning of the Church. "But now hath God set the members every one of them in the body, as it hath pleaseth him.

"And the eye cannot say unto the hand, I have no need of thee: nor again the head to the feet, I have no need of you.

"Now ye are the body of Christ, and members in particular.

"And God hath set some in the church, *first apostles, secondarily prophets,* thirdly teachers, after that miracles, then gifts of healings, helps, governments, diversity of tongues" (1 Corinthians 12:18,21,27-28).

God has organized His Church with certain offices and spiritual gifts to insure its temporal success and spiritual vitality. The Lord's Church is not organized by employing some offices and disregarding others through some random or multiple-choice methodology. All offices established by the Lord are essential to the proper functioning of His Church. None of them are superfluous or obsolete. Those today who profess that apostles and prophets are unnecessary appendages of the Church deny the wisdom of God by declaring, "The body has no need of the head."

By way of epistle, Paul told the Ephesians how long apostles and prophets were necessary to provide spiritual stability to the Church. "And *he [the Lord] gave some apostles; and some prophets;* and some evangelists; and some pastors and teachers;

"For the perfecting of the saints, for the work of the ministry, for the edifying of the body of Christ:

"*Till we all come in the unity of the faith,* and of the knowledge of the Son of God, unto a perfect man, unto the measure of the stature of the fullness of Christ:

"That we henceforth be no more children, tossed to and fro, and carried about with every wind of doctrine, by the sleight of men, and cunning craftiness, whereby they lie in wait to deceive" (Ephesians 4:11-14).

With the denominational diversity in existence today, and with so many varying interpretations of the scriptures, who could rightfully declare that the disciples of Jesus Christ have come to a "unity of the faith" or that God's children are no longer "carried about with every wind of doctrine?" That continuous divine revelation is essential to the spiritual health and well-being of the Church is manifested in the proliferation of doctrines espoused by the hundreds, possibly thousands, of Christian sects in existence today.

Who would dare say that we have no need of new revelation to guide us and teach us correct doctrine? In light of Paul's writings, it is evident that the present state of worldly affairs warrants the inspired leadership that only the "foundation of the apostles and prophets" can provide.

Elder Mark E. Petersen, a man chosen by the Lord to serve as a latter-day apostle, once said, "When there are no prophets, there is no divine direction, and without such guidance the people walk in darkness. It is an infallible sign of the true church that it has in it divinely chosen, living prophets to guide it, men who receive current revelation from God and whose recorded works become new scripture. It is an infallible sign of the true church also that it will produce new and additional scripture arising out of the ministrations of those prophets. This unfailing pattern of God is clearly made manifest through his dealings with his people from the beginning."[4]

MISUNDERSTOOD TEACHINGS ON REVELATION

Some people might assert that there can be no prophets today. Some use the following scripture in an attempt to strengthen their position: "God, who at sundry times and in diverse manners spake in time past unto the fathers by the prophets, hath in these last days spoken unto us by his Son" (Hebrews 1:1-2). Many advocates of this idea proclaim, "Christ was the last prophet; we are now guided by the scriptures and the Holy Ghost." This approach warrants closer scrutiny.

First, the New Testament speaks of many prophets who lived after the death and resurrection of Jesus Christ, such as Agabus, Judas, and Silas (Acts 13:1; 15:32; 21:10).

Second, the reference in the above scripture to the Son having spoken in the "last days" could be appropriately translated to read "most recent days." This letter was addressed to saints who lived in the first century, therefore from their point of view Christ had come in the most recent or these "last days."[5]

Third, the New Testament writings were recorded long after the death and resurrection of the Savior. If God has spoken to us in these last days by His Son, and if this is to mean that no further revelation or scripture was to be given after Christ, then we must dispose of the entire New Testament.

Fourth, in the past, God's children were not expected to depend solely on the promptings of the Holy Ghost or sacred writings of deceased prophets, nor were they to rely only on the utterances of living prophets for divine guidance. They enjoyed the blessings of all three. "For the prophecy came not in old time by the will of man: but holy men [prophets] of God spake as they were moved by the Holy Ghost" (2 Peter 1:21). Today, we are blessed with living prophets and inspired scriptures, as well as the Holy Ghost, just as God's children were anciently.

THE CONTINUING APOSTLESHIP

Latter-day Saints believe in the same organization that existed in the early Christian Church, of which, as the scriptures testify, apostles and prophets were an essential part. Christ chose twelve apostles, not only to preach His gospel during His own mortal ministry, but to perpetuate the Church after His death and resurrection as well. The apostles continued to receive instruction from the Lord by revelation, and worked arduously to prevent false doctrines from creeping into the Church.

For example, the chief apostle, Peter, received a vision instructing him that Christ's gospel should be preached to all people, to the Gentile as well the Jew, for "God is no respecter of persons" (Acts 10). Through the instrumentality of His chosen servants "the Lord added to the church daily" (Acts 2:47).

Since the twelve apostles were to serve the Church until "we all come in the unity of faith," the continuation of the apostleship was essential to the spiritual survival of the Church. However, upon Judas' death and prior betrayal, the Church's foundation of apostles was found lacking one apostle. Consequently, the other eleven apostles gathered together to choose his replacement by revelation. "And they appointed two, Joseph called Barsabas, who was surnamed Justus, and Matthias.

"And they prayed, and said, Thou, Lord, which knowest the hearts of all men, show whether of these two thou hast chosen,

"That he may take part of this ministry and apostleship, from which Judas by transgression fell, that he might go to his own place.

"And they gave forth their lots; and the lot fell upon Matthias; and he was numbered with the eleven apostles" (Acts 1:23-26).

This event plainly demonstrates that the Lord intended for the apostleship to continue in order that He might direct His Church by way of divine revelation. As further evidence, we know of many other men who were chosen as apostles, such as Barnabas, Paul (Acts 14:14), and the Lord's own brother, James (Galatians 1:19).

THE APOSTASY AND REVELATION

By the latter half of the first century, wickedness temporarily prevailed, as it often does, and the Lord's apostles were murdered one by one, most dying horrible deaths. Due to the long distances that separated them, they were unable to reconvene as a body of apostles to replace those who were killed in order to perpetuate the apostleship. As a result, the apostles dwindled in number until the last, John the Revelator, was no longer heard from.

The apostleship was lost from the earth due to the wickedness of man and not because of any design of God. Revelation, the mode of communication by which God directs His Church, died with the apostles, thus leading to the eventual demise of the true Church. This spiritual fall of the Church was prophesied by Paul, as he wrote to the saints in Thessalonica, "Let no man deceive you by any means: for that day [the Second Coming of Christ] shall not come, except there come a *falling away* first" (2 Thessalonians 2:3).

This falling away, or apostasy, as it is often called, was brought about by external persecution of the saints and internal corruption of Christ's true teachings. With the death of the guardians of the Church, the apostles, and the loss of divine revelation, spiritual darkness fell upon the Church, thus opening the door for one of history's darkest periods. Polycarp (A.D. 69-155), a bishop of Smyrna in Asia Minor who knew the Apostle John personally,[6] described the passing of the ancient apostles as the time when "the light went out."[7]

During the Dark Ages, as they are now appropriately known, all manner of atrocities were committed in the name of God. Men preferred darkness and lies to light and truth. Only a remnant of the gospel of Jesus Christ survived this 1,000 year period of spiritual ignorance, during which time the false teachings of Satan and the philosophies and creeds of men replaced many of the true teachings of the Savior.

Restoration Vs. Reformation

After a long millennial night of spiritual darkness, the dawning of a new gospel dispensation commenced with the appearance of our Heavenly Father and His Son, Jesus Christ, to Joseph Smith, a young man divinely chosen as the one through whom God would restore His kingdom on earth in the last days. In prior ages, God had chosen men such as Enoch, Noah, Abraham, and Moses, to restore His gospel truths and priesthood authority, direct His earthly affairs, and serve as instruments in His almighty hand. This sacred responsibility would now fall upon another man of similar spiritual stature, raised up by God for the purpose of restoring all that had been lost during the Dark Ages in preparation for the Second Coming of Jesus Christ.

As this chosen liaison between heaven and earth, Joseph Smith received priesthood authority — which is the privilege to act in behalf of the Lord — and divine instruction from heavenly messengers sent by God. On May 15, 1829, a resurrected John the Baptist appeared to Joseph Smith and Oliver Cowdery to restore to the earth the Aaronic, or Lesser, Priesthood, with all its attendant rights and privileges. Not many weeks later, the ancient apostles, Peter, James, and John, restored the Melchizedek, or Greater, Priesthood, thus granting Joseph Smith the authority with which he could later reestablish the Church of Jesus Christ on April 6, 1830.

On April 3, 1836, Moses conveyed to Joseph Smith the keys — that is, the power and authority — to preside over and conduct the gathering of Israel. On that same day, Elias committed the dispensation of the gospel of Abraham — the gospel of eternal marriage — and Elijah restored the keys of the power to seal families and generations together throughout eternity. These ancient apostles and prophets of God, along with other great religious personalities of the past, including Adam, Noah, and Paul, all appeared to Joseph Smith and others at various times appointed by God, in order to lay the groundwork for the promised "restitution of all things" prophesied by the Apostle Peter (Acts 3:21), thus preparing the Lord's people for the return of their Redeemer.

The Latter-day Saints soberly declare to the world that God has performed a great work of restoration, foreseen by many prophets of old, in which heavenly personages have communed with mortal men, called as prophets, conveying eternal truths and divine authority long lost from a disobedient and darkened world. Holy messengers of God, like Peter, James, and John, have indeed appeared to chosen, faithful mortals to restore all the powers, keys, doctrines, and authority necessary to bring to pass the eternal salvation of man, and to prepare all who would harken to this clarion call for the Second Coming of the Son of God, even Jesus Christ.

Too many important teachings of the Savior were lost or altered during the Dark Ages for a mere *reformation* to be adequate — a complete *restoration* of truths lost and authority removed was necessary to reestablish God's kingdom on earth. It is unprofitable to prune a dead tree; a new one must be planted in its place. For this reason, God chose to restore His redeeming gospel to the earth by way of heavenly messengers in this last dispensation of time, also known as the dispensation of the fulness of times. Every truth, principle, power, key, and authority necessary for the salvation of man from every past dispensation, as well as those reserved exclusively for this last dispensation, now exist on the earth today and reside within The Church of Jesus Christ of Latter-day Saints.

God is a loving God; He is our Heavenly Father. He does not want His children to forever live in darkness. It is for this reason that He saw fit to restore the truth and light of the gospel to the earth, once again establishing His Church upon a firm foundation of apostles and prophets. Once again, there is a living prophet who speaks in behalf of God as His chosen mouthpiece. Once again, there are twelve apostles that preach the gospel of Jesus Christ with power and authority. Once again, the fullness of the gospel is on the earth in all its wonder and simplicity. The Latter-day Saint message to the world is simple: the great Restoration of the gospel and kingdom of Jesus Christ has occurred as prophesied by prophets of centuries past. All are welcome to join the feast of gospel knowledge and eternal blessings that await those who desire to become the disciples of the Holy Lamb of God.

6

THE HOLY BIBLE

TRY to imagine a young family comprised of a newly-wed husband and wife just embarking on their journey together through life. Having only recently exchanged their marriage vows, they presently are childless; however, due to their love for children, they have plans for a large family.

Upon the arrival of their first child, they care for his every need. As loving parents concerned for his physical and spiritual welfare, they teach him good and correct principles by which he can live happily and prosperously. These loving parents teach their young child all that they have learned from their own experiences to help him become well-balanced and successful throughout his life. Most importantly, they teach him the plan of salvation that God has provided for his return to heaven to attain eternal life through the atonement of Jesus Christ.

They teach him certain rules of etiquette, courtesy, and civility in order that he can function in an orderly society. They teach him the fundamentals of nutrition, personal hygiene, grooming, and attire. They impress upon him the value of hard and honest work. They provide him with a proper education to prepare him for a career to support his own future family. They make all efforts to help him become self-sufficient, relying only on his Maker, in addition to his own talents and industry, for his survival.

This young man understands perfectly what his parents expect of him. They have communicated directly and clearly to their son the truths and instruction requisite for his temporal survival and spiritual well-being. They also encourage him to keep a journal to preserve his most memorable experiences and most valuable lessons for himself and his posterity. Throughout his life, he has received constant, day-to-day guidance from his loving parents until he is able to stand independent of all creatures under heaven.

As this young man continues to grow and progress, his parents fulfill their plans for a large family, bringing into the world many cherished sons and daughters. Each child receives the same loving care, attention, and guidance that the first child received. These conscientious parents tend to every detail in the rearing of their children, desiring that each gets a proper education and the firsthand instruction that their eldest child received.

The years go on and the family continues to grow. Eventually, these once-attentive parents become lax in their parental responsibilities. Perhaps they have grown tired of giving constant direction to their children, or perhaps they are simply unaware that their high standards of parenting have declined over the years. No longer willing to give their latest children the same care and guidance that the first received, the parents instruct the older children to keep a written record of everything they have learned from the father and mother. They are commanded to document their personal dealings with their parents, as well as all instruction relevant to their temporal and spiritual livelihood.

The parents have decided to spend little or no time with their latest children, since they feel this written record will serve to adequately supplant the direct supervision and influence the eldest children received from them. In other words, while the oldest siblings enjoyed the benefits and blessings of their parents' direct intervention in their lives as they grew up, the youngest children would now have to settle for a written account of that earlier nurturing. As the father and mother have taken an extended and unexplained leave of absence from the household, future parental advice would now come by book, rather than by word of mouth from the source.

This sufficed for awhile, but soon the younger children had questions regarding what was written. Some of the journal entries could be interpreted in more than one way. Order in the household wasn't too chaotic as long as some of the older children were still around to give advice and clarify the written record, but soon, none of the elder children, who communed directly with their parents in the past, were living in the same household. Some had moved away to attend college; some got married and started their own families. Some had even passed away.

The younger children became very confused without direct access to their parents. They even began to grow contentious as they argued over the correct interpretation of their elder siblings' notes. Certain words were no longer used by the younger generation, therefore they weren't sure of their meaning. In some cases, older entries were crossed out, and comments were added by later children, resulting in a multitude of revisions to the record.

Perhaps the greatest challenge was dealing with situations which had never occurred with any previous child in the family. The family records were simply silent on certain subjects and experiences. Since the mother and father were no longer around to give constant and direct instruction to their children, the youngest siblings were consigned to deal with these problems and challenges on their own. Consequently, the youngest kids suffered in both body and spirit. Many left the household looking for guidance elsewhere, often in unwholesome places. Some assumed they knew what the parents wanted them to do and paid a dear price for their mistakes. Others simply gave up in desperation. Some cursed their parents for abandoning them. Sadly enough, some even wondered whether their parents were still alive, as it had been so long since anyone had heard from or seen them. The household eventually fell into disunity and confusion without the constant, direct guidance of the parents.

If such is the tragedy of an earthly home wherein the parents neglect or abandon their children, imagine the consequences for a heavenly family. It is good to know that Heavenly Father doesn't run His household like these hypothetical parents. However, as a child, and later as a young man, I was taught that our Heavenly Father no longer talked to His children the way he did in ages past. Those that held such a view had a difficult time explaining to me why a just and loving Father, who didn't play favorites with His children, would be a full-time Father for some of His children and an absentee Father for others. I was taught that Heavenly Father gave direct revelation to His children who inhabited the earth in millennia past; however, for some unexplainable reason we must now settle for the scant writings of these ancient peoples for our guidance and direction. In other words, while the ancients had living oracles and written records, we must now settle for books alone.

THE BIBLE: A PORTION OF GOD'S WORD

The Latter-day Saints cherish the inspired records, like the Holy Bible, that God has bequeathed to us as an inheritance from past civilizations in order that we might learn from the experiences of those who preceded us. However, unlike the last children in the above hypothetical family, we do not believe that God expects His children to determine all truth and confront life's challenges armed only with a written record such as the Bible. While the history of God's dealings with our ancestors provides invaluable insights into daily living, it is no substitute for the day-to-day direction which comes from our Heavenly Father through the Holy Ghost and living prophets. For the

Latter-day Saints, the Bible represents only a portion of God's wisdom and instruction to His children — a mere fragment from among His many dealings with His chosen people throughout the world and throughout history. In other words, while the Bible constitutes inspired scripture, it does not constitute all scripture.

As Latter-day Saints, we believe that whatsoever the Lord's chosen prophets "shall speak when moved upon by the Holy Ghost shall be scripture, shall be the will of the Lord, shall be the mind of the Lord, shall be the word of the Lord, shall be the voice of the Lord, and the power of God unto salvation" (Doctrine & Covenants 68:4). In other words, any inspired revelation from God is scripture, for all divine inspiration is worthy of preservation as holy writ for the proper instruction of God's children. This broader definitional approach as to what constitutes scripture has profound implications for the LDS view toward the Holy Bible.

As Latter-day Saints, "we believe the Bible to be the word of God as far as it is translated correctly" (Eighth Article of Faith). (Reservations relating to the accuracy of the transmission of the Bible over the centuries will be discussed shortly). While Latter-day Saints believe the Bible to contain the inspired word of God, we do not insist that it constitutes the only word of God. Latter-day Saints recognize the prerogative of the living, almighty God to grant further revelation and inspire additional scripture as the great work of saving His children moves forward.

As previously stated, the Latter-day Saints do not believe that the Holy Bible is the only word of God, nor do they believe that it contains all gospel truth essential to the salvation of man, nor that, in its present condition, it is free from tampering by uninspired scribes. The popular belief in a closed canon ignores many pertinent biblical scriptures, historical facts, recent textual discoveries, and early Christian writings. Before we limit God's word to the 39 books of the Old Testament and the 27 books of the New Testament, rejecting further light and knowledge from God, perhaps we should consider how the biblical canon evolved over the centuries before it was finally handed down to the current generation of believers in its present form.

The very title of the Bible has led to much confusion and has contributed to the difficulty many people have in accepting scripture beyond the biblical canon. Most people think of "the Bible" as a single book or volume of scripture, however the English term "Bible" actually derives from the Greek plural term "Biblia" which literally means "books." The Bible should not be thought of as a solitary volume, for it is actually a collection or library of sacred texts written over a period spanning thousands of years. It wasn't until much later that this continually expanding assortment of sacred "books" began to be combined under one cover, and later still, probably during the thirteenth century, that the Latin derivative of "Biblia" came to be known as the singular noun, "Book."[1] This incorrect usage of the term "Bible," which evolved during the Dark Ages, promotes the misconception that this compilation of sacred writings has always existed as a closed, static, and complete volume to which no new revelation should be added, a notion known to be contrary to the beliefs of early Christians.

It is not difficult to understand why Christians of the era of spiritual darkness following the death of the apostles considered the canon closed, living during a time of revelatory drought. A church deprived of any divine revelations from God for centuries would naturally come to the conclusion that God must be finished communicating with His children. Desiring to assure its continued temporal survival long after its spiritual vitality had passed, early Christians must have recognized the necessity of embracing some collection of inspired documents from among those still available, as proxy for God's authority and inspiration. Unfortunately, many today have unquestioningly accepted the decisions made by the turbulent and heated councils of the fourth and fifth centuries as the final word on the contents of our present-day New Testament canon.

There are at least three general reasons why the orthodox belief in the Bible as the exclusive and unadulterated word of God is not accepted by the Latter-day Saints. First, not all inspired Hebrew or Christian writings are found in our modern-day Bible. Second, not all teachings conveyed by the Lord to His disciples, nor by His prophets and apostles, were recorded and included in the Bible. Third, many passages of the Bible have been removed from the original inspired text or have been altered since their original transmission. Each of these points will now be discussed in greater detail.

NOT ALL INSPIRED WRITINGS ARE FOUND IN THE BIBLE

Non-Biblical Prophetic Writings

Many portions of the various books which constitute our current Bible have been lost or removed over the centuries. Many discoveries of ancient records have produced copies of biblical writings that predate the manuscript copies that have heretofore served as the basis for modern biblical translations. For example, the Dead Sea Scrolls contain the entire book of Isaiah and portions of every other Old Testament book except Ruth,[2] in addition to more than 300 other books currently not found in the Bible. Comparisons with these older records reveal that much of the original content of our most cherished biblical books is missing from our current editions of the Bible.

Writing on this particular subject, William F. Albright, perhaps the world's most prominent biblical archaeologist, stated, "Our Hebrew text has suffered much more from losses than from glosses." After providing a number of examples, he writes in the Journal of Bible and Religion that "future translations will have to expand the text substantially — including...some [passages] of great importance for their content."[3] Many biblical scholars agree that future translations of the Bible will warrant substantial text expansion to incorporate these previously missing passages.

Thousands of ancient records, many of which are believed to be prophetic, have come forth in the past several decades. Many of these valuable finds carry with them claimed authorship by Christ's ancient apostles, such as the "Apocryphon of John," "The Apocalypse of Paul," the "Apocalypse of James," "The Gospel of Philip," and the "Apocalypse of Peter," to name a few. These ancient records have forced scholars and theologians of all denominations to change their way of thinking relative to the daily operations of the early Christian Church and the previously supposed exclusivity of the Bible.

Our modern-day New Testament includes writings of only five of the known apostles of the early Church. It would not be presumptuous for us to ask what happened to the writings of the other apostles. And what of the many great Old Testament prophets such as Adam, Enoch, Noah, Abraham, Isaac, Jacob, and Joseph? Were their pens barren or have their writings simply been lost or hidden from mankind? As previously stated, recent archaeological discoveries seem to indicate the latter, as more and more ancient writings are being found, many of which claim divine origins as penned by New Testament personalities like John, Peter, Paul, Philip, Thomas, and Barnabas, to name a few.

As for the Old Testament patriarch, Abraham, some of his inspired writings have been restored in these latter days for all mankind to read, through the instrumentality of the Prophet Joseph Smith.

The Bible itself mentions many ancient scriptural writings that were at one time accessible but are now lost to mankind. The Bible testifies of such inspired writings as the book of Gad the seer (1 Chronicles 29:29), book of Nathan the prophet (1 Chronicles 29:29; 2 Chronicles 9:29), prophecy of Ahijah (2 Chronicles 9:29), sayings of the seers (2 Chronicles 33:19), an epistle from the Apostle Paul to the Corinthians earlier than 1 Corinthians (1 Corinthians 5:9), and another Pauline epistle to the saints of ancient Laodicea (Colossians 4:16). The Bible cannot possibly be the complete word of God, since other inspired writings containing the words of God exist that are not included in our modern versions of this sacred text. (See also Exodus 24:7; Numbers 21:14; Joshua 10:13; 1 Samuel 10:25; 2 Chronicles 12:15; 13:22; 20:34).

The Canonization of the Scriptures

During the first several centuries following the Savior's death and resurrection, many of the books and epistles which constituted what is known today as the New Testament were highly disputed. As councils of uninspired men attempted to differentiate between inspired and man-made writings, the contents of the New Testament changed frequently until around A.D.400.[4] Various books and letters were added or removed according to the doctrinal whim of the day.

According to J.N.D. Kelly, "the fixation of the finally agreed list of books, and of the order in which they were to be arranged, was the result of a very gradual process. While the broad outline of the canon was settled by the end of the second century, different localities continued to maintain their different traditions, and some appear to have been less partial to fixity than others...The first official document which prescribes the twenty-seven books of our New Testament as alone canonical is Athanasius's Easter Letter for the year 367, but the process was not everywhere complete until at least a century and a half later."[5]

Harry Y. Gamble, Associate Professor of Religious Studies at the University of Virginia, writes: "...the NT [New Testament] was not an original or even a particularly early feature of Christianity. Rather, the NT [New Testament] developed only gradually over the course of several centuries, as the result of a complex variety of conditioning factors in the life of the ancient church, and did not attain the form in which we know it until the late fourth century."[6] He later writes, "The documents which were eventually to become distinctively Christian scriptures were written for immediate and practical purposes within the early churches, and only gradually did they come to be valued and to be spoken of as 'scripture'."[7]

Just as the doctrine of the Godhead was debated by uninspired men centuries after wicked men persecuted and killed the prophets and apostles, the development of the scriptural canon underwent a similar process. The men that convened in these church councils were not prophets or apostles, nor were they guided by the Holy Ghost. They were guided by their own fallible intellect, and, as a result, their councils were characterized by debate, contention, and confusion.

On this topic, Professor Gamble writes, "Again, the history of the canon, like the history of the ancient church generally, shows the effects of the political rivalries, cultural differences, and theological orientations of the great centers of ecclesiastical influence: above all, Rome, Alexandria, and Antioch...And, so far as canonization is understood strictly as the determination of a fixed and closed list of authoritative scriptures, official ecclesiastical decisions rendered by bishops or councils must be given their due."[8] The relevant point made by Latter-day Saints is that the scriptures were altered and canonized during a period of spiritual darkness and confusion as evidenced by the practices and teachings of these misguided custodians of an apostate church, as well as the uninspired decisions of their divisive councils.

To complicate the matter even more, different ecclesiastical councils approved different compilations of books. What was considered inspired by one group was considered heretical by another. By the late fourth century, an official canon of New Testament writings gained predominance over all other contending scripture lists, ultimately achieving universal acceptance through its continued use over time. "A broad uniformity of usage which closely approximates our NT [New Testament] cannot therefore be dated before the close of the fourth century...this emergent uniformity was fundamentally de facto, for no ecumenical authority of the ancient church ever rendered a formal decision for the church at large as to the exact contents of Christian scripture."[9]

The New Testament that has been handed down to us today is the word of God, nevertheless it does not include certain writings such as the "Revelation of Peter," "The Teaching of the Twelve Apostles," "The Shepherd of Hermas," "Clement I," the "Epistle of Barnabas," "The Gospel of the Hebrews," or a number of other writings which were considered inspired scripture during the first two centuries following Christ's resurrection. Ironically, our modern New Testament does include epistles and books such as James, 3 John, 2 Peter, Hebrews, and Revelation, which were not recognized as canonical scripture by Christians of the first two to three centuries.[10] As for the Old Testament, this collection of ancient prophetic books as we currently know them was not settled upon until the 17th Century.

Essentially, what modern Christians consider the Holy Bible is not necessarily what earlier Christians had in mind. According to Professor Gamble of the University of Virginia, "...there is no intimation at all that the early church entertained the idea of Christian scriptures, much less a collection of them. Therefore, the NT [New Testament] as we think of it was utterly remote from the minds of the first generations of Christian believers."[11]

The Post-Apostolic Salvage Effort

The early Christian historical record reveals that the collection of assorted writings that currently comprises the New Testament does not contain the entire written account of the Savior's or apostles' teachings. Consider the matter of the four New Testament Gospels: Matthew, Mark, Luke, and John. These Gospels were essentially intended to serve as testimonies that Jesus is the Christ, the Only Begotten Son of God, and the Savior of the world. However, early Christian writers refer to many other gospels used as scripture by the early Church besides the four currently found in the New Testament. Recent manuscript discoveries have turned up the likes of the "Gospel of Thomas," "Gospel of Peter," "Gospel of the Hebrews," and "Dialogue of the Savior."[12] During the first two centuries, these Gospels and others were commonly used by early Christians, indicating that the four which came to be canonized were neither unique in content nor did they possess some special authority over the other gospels. As for the Gospel of John, it appears that it was not known or used by most second-century Christian writers.[13]

As for Paul's writings, most of his epistles were responses to specific questions and issues within the first-century Church. "Paul's letters were practical expedients of his missionary work: addressed to specific churches, they are narrowly particular in substance and purpose and make no pretense of general interest or timeless relevance...Since each of Paul's letters was an ad hoc piece of correspondence written to a specific church and dealing with immediate and local issues, it is not obvious that an enduring value would have been seen in them even by their original recipients, much less by other churches."[14] Paul's epistles contribute wonderful insights into select Christian doctrines and practices, yet they must be understood in the proper historical and cultural context lest they be misinterpreted.

As it became increasingly more apparent that the light of revelation that guided the first-century Church had dimmed with the passing of the apostles, church leaders of subsequent centuries made efforts to gather the inspired writings that were still accessible in an attempt to salvage the teachings of the Savior and His apostles, thereby clinging to any vestige of evidence of the early Church's spiritual vitality and glory.[15] "The passage of time, the demise of the apostles, and the dissipation of oral tradition both led to the composition of Christian writings and elevated their importance as means of sustaining the church's relationship to the decisive events of its origins."[16] While many valuable revelations, testimonies, and epistles were gathered, many others were lost. Despite the valiant scavenging efforts of these primarily second- through fourth-century Christians, it was too little and too late.

As for limiting our New Testament to the letters and testimonies which now constitute its contents, one modern Christian scholar sums it up this way: "In the light of modern knowledge about the history of the canon and the character of its contents, it is difficult to justify the limitation of the canon to precisely the twenty-seven documents which have traditionally belonged to it...As the canon took shape, only such documents as had survived and were still available could be considered for inclusion in it. But some of Paul's letters, the written sources behind the Gospels, and no doubt many other pieces of early Christian literature were simply lost. In this sense, the potential content of the canon was affected from the outset by the accidents of literary preservation." The impact of "historical circumstances, theological controversies, traditions of interpretation, regional usages, judgments of ecclesiastical authorities, and even the technical aspects of book manufacture and textual transmission" also influenced the long formative process and final outcome of the New Testament canon.[17]

THE BIBLE DOES NOT CONTAIN ALL OF CHRIST'S TEACHINGS

Unrecorded Revelation and Instruction

In addition to that which was lost or removed, the Bible does not include that which the Lord and His ancient apostles chose not to record in the first place. The apostles taught much by word of mouth rather than by epistle (2 Thessalonians 2:15). "The apostles wrote only under the pressure of external circumstances; even in later times, living oral instruction remained the regular means of transmission and propagation of the Christian truth."[18]

Tertullian, a second-century Christian, wrote, "We believe that the apostles were ignorant of nothing, but that they did not transmit everything they knew, and were not willing to reveal everything to everybody. They did not preach everywhere nor promiscuously."[19]

If one were to read all of the Savior's direct quotes found in the

New Testament, the task could be accomplished quite easily in a half hour. We know that Christ preached for approximately three years prior to His crucifixion, yet the Bible has only preserved 30 minutes of His sermons. Surely the Savior did and said many things which are not recorded for any man or woman to read, for "if they should be written every one, I suppose that even the world itself could not contain the books that should be written" (John 21:25). The Apostle John also testifies, "And many other signs truly did Jesus in the presence of his disciples, which are not written in this book" (John 20:30).

The 27 books and letters which comprise today's New Testament do not address the full range of gospel doctrines with which early Church members were familiar. Many of the doctrines which were taught by word of mouth (2 Thessalonians 2:15) remained unrecorded. Many other teachings were withheld until the saints were spiritually prepared to receive them (1 Corinthians 3:2). On this particular matter, Clement of Rome, the first-century bishop, credits the Apostle Peter with saying, "The teaching of all doctrine has a certain order: there are some things which must be delivered first, others in the second place, and others in the third, and so on, everything in its order. If these things be delivered in their order they become plain; but if they be brought forward out of order, they will seem to be spoken against reason."[20]

Expounding on the teachings imparted by Christ's ancient apostles, Clement of Alexandria, a second-century Christian scholar, wrote, "Which things were plainly spoken but are not plainly written."[21] The Oxford theology scholar, J.N.D. Kelly, adds, "There is no reason to infer, however, that the primitive Church regarded the apostolic testimony as confined to written documents emanating from, or attributed to, the apostles. Logically, as it must have done chronologically, the [spoken] testimony stood prior to the documents."[22] A most powerful witness on this matter comes down to us from Clement of Rome, who testified that the ancient apostles "gave little thought to writing anything down."[23]

Where in the Bible do we find the teachings or writings of Christ's original apostles such as Andrew, Philip, Nathanael, Thomas, Jude, Judas, James the less, or Simon the Canaanite? What of the men who were later called to the holy apostleship, such as Barnabas and Matthias? As for Paul and the remaining apostles, Clement says they "left nothing in writing but a few extremely short letters."[24]

The Savior's 40-Day Post-Resurrection Ministry

Immediately following His resurrection, the Savior returned to His apostles, "being seen of them forty days, and speaking of the things pertaining to the kingdom of God" (Acts 1:3). During this 40-day ministry, the Lord did not return to simply repeat things He had already taught His apostles. He returned to convey "higher" gospel doctrines which He had never revealed during His mortal ministry.

Prior to His crucifixion, Christ told His apostles, "I have yet many things to say unto to you, but ye cannot bear them now. Howbeit when he, the Spirit of truth, is come, he will guide you into all truth" (John 16:12-13). These higher teachings of the gospel needed to be conveyed to the apostles, as they do to all mankind, by the power of the Spirit in order to be properly understood (1 Corinthians 2:13-14).

It is also critical that the fundamentals of the gospel of Jesus Christ are comprehended before Church members are spiritually prepared to receive the profounder doctrines of the gospel (Isaiah 28:9-10; 1 Corinthians 3:2; Hebrews 5:12). Since the Comforter could not "come unto" the apostles until after the death of Christ (John 16:7), they were not spiritually prepared to receive "the things pertaining to the kingdom of God" until Christ's post-resurrection return. At this later time, the Savior "through the Holy Ghost had given commandments unto the apostles whom he had chosen" (Acts 1:2).

On this subject, the second-century Church historian, Eusebius quotes an even earlier Christian, Clement of Rome: "To James the Just and to John and Peter after the resurrection of the Lord conveyed the gnosis [not to be confused with the false gnosis, or knowledge, claimed by the Gnostics], these handed it on to the rest of the Apostles and in turn to the Seventy."[25] And what was this knowledge that was conveyed to the apostles by the Lord after His resurrection? "These things are more marvellous than what we were taught before." "Now he teaches us things which we had not known before, great, amazing, and real things." Ancient texts such as the Apocryphon of James, Apocryphon of John, and Acts of Thomas, reveal that the apostles, for the first time, learned "the ultimate secrets" or "the highest knowledge."[26]

As important as these teachings were, our modern-day Bible remains almost totally silent on the wondrous doctrines Christ revealed to His apostles during this 40-day ministry. These sacred teachings were reserved for the spiritually prepared and initiated, not the world at large, for the "teaching of all doctrine has a certain order."

The Bible Testifies of Continuous Revelation

The Bible itself is evidence of continuous revelation. The Bible records God's firsthand dealings with man from Adam to John the Revelator. During this entire period of 4,000 years, save a few short periods of apostasy due to Israel's disobedience, God spoke to His children through chosen, living prophets. Without prophets and continuing revelation there would have been no Bible.

As for the exclusivity of the Bible, nowhere within its inspired pages does the Bible make the claim that it is the only word of God. In fact, the very existence of hundreds of different Christian denominations indicates that the Bible alone is not sufficient to establish doctrinal or organizational unity.

MANY BIBLICAL PASSAGES HAVE BEEN ALTERED OR REMOVED

Biblical Manuscripts

In light of the overwhelming and still-accumulating evidence, modern biblical scholars are almost unanimous in their agreement that many biblical passages have been altered, either accidentally or deliberately. Among the thousands of existing copies of Greek manuscripts of the New Testament, there are approximately 150,000 places in which there are variant readings.[27] Not a single one of these manuscripts is the original; all of them are copies of copies of copies with the earliest complete manuscript dating to the fourth century after Christ. There is much evidence of deletions, additions, and commentary inscribed directly on the manuscripts themselves. Even as early as the second century, the Christian scholar, Origen, had this to say concerning the scriptural manuscripts: "Today the fact is evident, that there are many differences in the manuscripts, either through the negligence of certain copyists, or the perverse audacity of some in correcting the text."[28]

Eerdmans' Handbook to the History of Christianity states, "The overwhelming mass of variations in the many manuscripts studied consist of accidental spelling differences or omissions. But some variations are clearly deliberate. Most of these appear to be attempts to 'improve' the style, to remove ambiguity or sometimes to harmonize parallel accounts in different books. A few of the variations appear to be caused by a copyist's concern about doctrine...Though the writings were considered important, this did not always guarantee scrupulous, exact copying of them. While no manuscript is free of either accidental or deliberate variations, some manuscripts seem to reflect a more careful tradition of copying, while others reveal a much freer attitude towards the actual words of the New Testament...Translations were not always prepared by people with a good command of Greek, and are often very imperfect."[29]

In reference to the epistles of Paul, Professor Gamble writes that "most scholars are prepared to grant that secondary editorial revision has affected some of the letters."[30] With regard to 2 Corinthians in particular, which many scholars believe was pieced together from smaller fragments, he indicates that "some letters were lost, some preserved, some extensively edited, and some newly composed."[31] As for the Gospels, there appeared to be "a more general tendency in the second century not to regard the texts of Gospels as sacrosanct but to subject them to revisions of various types."[32]

Biblical Translations

Most casual readers of the Bible rarely take the time to read the preface written by the translators to the reader, however these short summaries of translating methodology can prove extremely enlightening. Often the preface will refer the reader to shortcomings of previous versions of the Bible, thereby justifying the most current translation project. Also, the translating committee typically recognizes difficulties and discusses imperfections in its own translation, as the following examples illustrate.

The translators of the 1611 King James Version of the Bible made many comments regarding the Septuagint, the Greek translation of the Old Testament commonly used by early Christians, that shed light on its reliability. "It is certaine, that that Translation was not so sound and so perfect, but that it needed in many places correction...the Seventie [who translated the Septuagint] were Interpreters, they were not Prophets; they did many things well, as learned men; but yet as men they stumbled and fell, one while through oversight, another while through ignorance, yea, sometimes they may be noted to adde to the Originall, and sometimes to take from it...The translation of the Seventie dissenteth from the Originall in many places, neither doeth it come neere it, for perspicuitie, gravitie, maiestie; yet which of the Apostles did condemne it? Condemne it? Nay, they used it."

Then speaking of their own translating accomplishment, the King James Version, the translators expressed hope: "...if we building upon their foundation that went before us, and being holpen by their labours, doe endevour to make that better which they left so good; no man, we are sure, hath cause to mislike us..."[33]

The King James translators recognized the popular Septuagint as the word of God despite its imperfections introduced through ignorance and mischief. Their admirable quest was to improve upon the work of their predecessors, bringing biblical scripture closer to the original revelations of God. This has been the ultimate goal of every Bible translating committee since that time.

According to its preface, "The Revised Standard Version [1952] of the Bible is an authorized revision of the American Standard Version, published in 1901, which was a revision of the King James Version, published in 1611." Just as the King James translators found fault with the Septuagint, the translators of the Revised Standard Version justified their efforts by noting imperfections in the King James Version. "Yet the King James Version has grave defects. By the middle of the nineteenth century, the development of Biblical studies and the discovery of many manuscripts more ancient than those upon which the King James Version was based, made it manifest that these defects are so many and so serious as to call for revision of the English translation...The King James Version of the New Testament was based upon a Greek text that was marred by mistakes, containing the accumulated errors of fourteen centuries of manuscript copying...We now possess many more ancient manuscripts of the New Testament, and are far better equipped to seek to recover the original wording of the Greek text."

The RSV translators then discuss their own problems with the translation process and the manner in which they manage these problems: "For the New Testament we have a large number of Greek manuscripts, preserving many variant forms of the text...it seems clear that errors in copying had been made before the text was standardized...Sometimes it is evident that the text has suffered in transmission, but none of the versions provides a satisfactory restoration. Here we can only follow the best judgment of competent scholars as to the most probable reconstruction of the original text...Many difficulties and obscurities, of course, remain...If in the judgment of the Committee the meaning of a passage is quite uncertain or obscure, either because of corruption in the text or because of the inadequacy of our present knowledge of the language, that fact is indicated by a note...Some changes of words or phrases are made in the interest of consistency, clarity, or accuracy of translation."[34]

Having admitted the shortcomings of the surviving ancient manuscripts, previous Biblical versions, and their own translation effort, the Committee members unite in voice with their noble predecessors: "We are glad to say, with the King James translators: 'Truly (good Christian Reader) we never thought from the beginning, that we should need to make a new Translation, nor yet to make of a bad one a good one…but to make a good one better."[35]

One of the most popular versions of the Bible today is the New International Version published in 1973. "The New International Version is a completely new translation of the Holy Bible made by over a hundred scholars working directly from the best available Hebrew, Aramaic, and Greek texts…For the Old Testament the standard Hebrew text, the Masoretic Text as published in the latest editions of Biblia Hebraica, was used throughout. The Dead Sea Scrolls contain material bearing on an earlier stage of the Hebrew text. They were consulted…"

Like their forerunners, the translators of this version were confronted with incredible challenges. "Because thought patterns and syntax differ from language to language, faithful communication of the meaning of the writers of the Bible demands frequent modifications in sentence structure and constant regard for the contextual meanings of words…They tried to reflect the differing styles of the biblical writers…Sometimes a variant Hebrew reading in the margin of the Masoretic Text was followed instead of the text itself…Readings from these versions [such as the Septuagint] were occasionally followed where the Masoretic Text seemed doubtful and where accepted principles of textual criticism showed that one or more of these textual witnesses appeared to provide the correct reading…Where existing manuscripts differ, the translators made their choice of readings according to accepted principles of New Testament textual criticism. Footnotes call attention to places where there was uncertainty about what the original text was.

"As in other ancient documents, the precise meaning of the biblical texts is sometimes uncertain. This is more often the case with the Hebrew and Aramaic texts than with the Greek text. Although archaeological and linguistic discoveries in this century aid in understanding difficult passages, some uncertainties remain…To achieve clarity, the translators sometimes supplied words not in the original texts but required by the context…In some cases two possible translations were considered to have about equal validity. In other cases, though the translators were convinced that the translation in the text was correct, they judged that another interpretation was possible and of sufficient importance to be represented in a footnote."[36] After identifying their numerous challenges and stumblingblocks, the NIV translators had this to say about their final product: "Like all translations of the Bible, made as they are by imperfect man, this one undoubtedly falls short of its goals."

The preceding comments made by these translating committees reveal that those who are most familiar with the ancient manuscripts are in a better position than the average student of the Bible to judge the integrity of the modern-day translations of the scriptures. The translators make it known in no uncertain terms that they are imperfect men and women conducting an imperfect work using imperfect resources to render an imperfect product. Regarding their resources, they talk of defects, mistakes, errors, and corruptions in the ancient manuscripts. They express the challenges in dealing with variant readings and forms, and differences in the manuscripts themselves. They discuss the obstacles imposed by certain passages which possibly have more than one interpretation, forcing them to rely on their own human intellect to determine the correct reading.

Concerning their own qualifications, the translators admit they are imperfect men and women, interpreters at best, and surely not prophets, limited in their efforts to the best in textual knowledge and criticism the schools of mankind currently have to offer. They confess to lacking certain needed understanding of the ancient biblical languages. Above all, they admit the entire translation process is characterized by an element of uncertainty.

Clearly, in its present condition, the Bible is far from perfect, for reasons the translating committees have amply described. Corruptions have been introduced into the once unblemished word of God over the centuries by careless custodians of the ancient scriptures, yet the tireless men and women who have labored to restore and clarify the word of God should be commended for their valiant efforts.

An important principle can be learned from the words of the various translating committees. Each committee recognizes the imperfections and shortcomings of previous translations, providing it with the magnanimous purpose of retranslating the holy word of God. Each committee implies by its actions superiority to previous efforts due to their access to more recent archaeological discoveries and improved textual understanding. Each translation implies to be an improvement over prior translations or the undertaking would not have been attempted.

What then is to prevent us from believing that future discoveries will render even better or more accurate translations than are presently offered? If a past translation was good, and a more recent one is better, when will a committee yet to be assembled provide Christendom with the absolute best, or even perfect, translation? The translating committee for the New International Version addressed this very issue when it wrote, "There is a sense in which the work of translation is never wholly finished."[37]

The insightful testimonies of the translating committees them-selves confirm that our present Bible translations are incomplete, imperfect, and, most importantly, short of the divine revelations originally conveyed by the Lord to His chosen prophets. Undoubtedly, modern-day Christians will continue to search the past in hopes of discovering prophetic glimpses into the future. Despite archaeology's valuable contributions to biblical scholarship, it is unfortunate to see followers of Christ exploring the ruins of past civilizations hoping to find eternal truths revealed thousands of years ago to holy men called to be prophets, when God has rolled back the heavens once again in our day to reveal these and greater truths to a new generation of divinely chosen men who go unheeded by the world at large.

The Causes of Scriptural Corruptions

It is not difficult to imagine what could happen over a 1,000-year period of spiritual darkness. Before the advent of the printing press, copies of the scriptures were made by quill and candlelight, every word of the Bible laboriously transcribed by hand. Could the copyist possibly make a mistake under these unfavorable conditions?

Consider the translator's incredible task of taking a document written in ancient Hebrew, Aramaic, or Greek, and translating it into a more modern language. All of the ancient manuscripts were written in languages that no one speaks today. In addition, it is almost impossible to find any two words in any two languages that share a perfect correlation. Given these linguistic challenges, any translation is merely an opinion at best. As one learned translator put it, "A translation is a statement in the translator's own words of what he thinks the author had in mind."[38] This is a monumental task when the original author lived hundreds or even thousands of years ago.

The difficulties faced by the translators employed by King James in the early part of the seventeenth century provide a perfect case in point. Even the casual reader of the King James Version of the Bible will notice that virtually thousands of words are italicized. These words have been printed in italics for at least one of two reasons. First, in order to translate certain concepts or ideas from ancient Greek or Hebrew to modern English, it is necessary to add certain words to properly convey the same thought. These added words were chosen by the translators; they were not part of the original text.

Secondly, due to numerous errors and ambiguities within the ancient manuscripts, some translators evidently felt obligated to use additional words in order to clarify the ideas they believed the original authors were attempting to communicate.[39] In other words, the translators exercised a certain amount of textual freedom in the translation process. In either case, they should be commended for their honesty in highlighting those words which were not found in the original texts.

Subsequent translating committees have been less open in this respect. Given the approximately 4,600 different and varying manuscripts from which to choose and the numerous biblical translating committees assembled over the centuries each with its own doctrinal leanings, is it any wonder why so many different translations of the Bible exist today?

Finally, consider the priest of the post-apostolic period, living at a time of spiritual decline when only the clergy is trusted with copies of the scriptures and common believers are deprived access to the written word of God. It is the commencement of the Dark Ages, that Black Millennium in which darkness shrouds the minds of men and the light of the gospel has given way to the shadows of ignorance. This is a time when men are killed in the name of God, when priesthood offices are positions of power purchased with money, doctrines are decided by ecclesiastical leaders whose vices know no bounds, and the scriptures are under the care of men devoid of the Holy Spirit of God.

As the priest of the post-apostolic era peruses the holy scriptures, he discovers a passage that is in blatant opposition to his own perception of truth. With a single stroke of the pen, the passage is gone or changed forever. He knows it is much easier to delete passages than to add them, as an attempt to duplicate holy writ would pose a greater challenge. However, he also knows that a strategically placed word or two can conveniently change the entire meaning of a passage.

Rufinus, a fourth-century monastic priest, while translating early Christian texts, admitted to leaving entire passages out that he personally found peculiar or contrary to his notion of proper Christian doctrine.[40]

Is it so hard to imagine a misguided priest, who lived during a time when ecclesiastical machinations did not preclude the use of murder, torture, bribery, or extortion, being capable of committing an act as simple as altering the scriptures to serve his own interests? Not only was he capable of it, but it was his "moral" duty to correct or delete any passage which his conscience dictated as heresy.[41] Perhaps in his own darkened mind, he did it for God, church, and country, an attitude undoubtedly shared by many of those who participated in the purges of the Holy Lands during the infamous Christian Crusades.

Many might assert that God would never permit His scriptures to be corrupted by man. However, has not God allowed His chosen prophets to be killed throughout the ages? Did not God allow His chosen apostles to be brutally killed by vicious murderers? Did He not permit His Beloved Son, Jesus Christ, to be humiliated, tortured, and killed by wicked men?

If He would allow His Only Begotten Son to be murdered, why is it so hard to believe that He would allow the scriptures to be corrupted as well? If He would allow Christ's chosen apostles, those who received divine revelation to guide the Church, to be removed from the midst of His people, then why wouldn't He allow the scriptures to be altered by corrupt men? After all, what is more important, living prophets or the writings of dead prophets? If given the choice between having a man such as Paul in our midst or simply a selection of his writings, which would you choose — the man or his letters?

It is crucial to realize that God grants man the freedom to choose his own course. If man chooses to kill the prophets rather than heed their words, the Lord allows it to happen. Likewise, if man chooses to corrupt God's word rather than abide by it in its purity, God will allow it. God is not threatened by man's feeble acts; man cannot foil God's plans. He has power to restore all that is lost due to man's carelessness or disobedience, however, come judgment time, all mankind will receive the just rewards of their actions.

Manmade Errors in the Bible

Perhaps a few examples of textual errors and inconsistencies will serve to demonstrate the improprieties man has taken with the scriptures over the ages. Keep in mind that these examples are not intended to lessen one's confidence in the scriptures, but to increase one's understanding of the Bible.

While traveling to Damascus, Paul was visited by the resurrected Savior Himself, "and the men which journeyed with him stood speechless, *hearing a voice,* but seeing no man" (Acts 9:7). Later, while recounting his story, Paul said, "And they that were with me saw indeed the light, and were afraid; but *they heard not the voice* of him that spake to me" (Acts 22:9). In one account his companions heard the voice, and in the other they did not — obviously a slight contradiction exists in the text.

There are many contradictions within the parallel accounts of the ministry of the Savior as recorded in the four gospels. Each of the four gospel writers give a different account of the words of the inscription that was placed over the Savior's head while he suffered on the cross (Matthew 27:37; Mark 15:26; Luke 23:38; John 19:19). When Mary Magdalene returned to the sepulchre where Christ was buried, according to Matthew and Mark she was greeted by *one angel* (Matthew 28:2-5; Mark 16:5), while Luke and John record that she was greeted by *two angels* (Luke 24:4-5; John 20:12-13).

Regarding the timing of the crucifixion, Luke records that Christ was *on the cross at the sixth hour* (Luke 23:44), yet according to John, *Pilate was presenting Christ to the angry Jews at the sixth hour* (John 19:14). As for Mark, he records the hour of the crucifixion as the third hour (Mark 15:25). These are just a few of the many existing discrepancies among the parallel gospel records.

Matthew writes that it was the prophet Jeremy (Jeremiah) that prophesied that the Savior would be betrayed for 30 pieces of silver (Matthew 27:9-10), yet the Old Testament reveals that it was actually the prophet Zechariah (Zechariah 11:12). If Jeremiah also made this prophecy, it is absent from our current Bible.

Consider the Savior's remarks to his disciples regarding great blessings to be granted to certain faithful followers:

"Verily I say unto you, There be some standing here, which shall not taste of death, till they see the Son of man coming in his kingdom" (Matthew 16:28).

"...Verily I say unto you, That there be some of them that stand here, which shall not taste of death, till they have seen the kingdom of God come with power" (Mark 9:1).

"But I tell you of a truth, there be some standing here, which shall not taste of death, till they see the kingdom of God" (Luke 9:27).

This statement made by the Savior is given three variant readings by three different biblical authors. The chronology of events before and after this quote show that all three writers are describing the same experience in the life of the Savior. This statement was preceded by Christ's entry into the coasts of Caesarea Philippi and followed by His incredible experience on the Mount of Transfiguration. While the message of each version of His statement is basically consistent, the words are not identical. At best, only one of the above scriptures accurately represents the Lord's actual statement. The most likely explanation is that His original words have not been handed down to us over the centuries in their original and untampered form, or perhaps they have suffered during the translation process. The original transmissions undoubtedly agreed since all three gospel accounts were recorded by men who were guided by the Holy Spirit of revelation.

The next example reveals even greater variation in the recording of specific words spoken by the Savior at a specific time in His ministry. In this particular setting, Jesus Christ has just been asked by Caiaphas, the Jewish high priest, whether He is indeed the Messiah, the Son of God:

"Jesus saith unto him, *Thou hast said:* nevertheless I say unto you, Hereafter shall ye see the Son of man sitting on the right hand of power, and coming in the clouds of heaven" (Matthew 26:64).

"And Jesus said, *I am:* and ye shall see the Son of man sitting on the right hand of power, and coming in the clouds of heaven" (Mark 14:62).

"And he said unto them, *If I tell you, ye will not believe:* And if I also ask you, ye will not answer me, nor let me go. Hereafter shall the Son of man sit on the right hand of the power of God" (Luke 22:67-69).

It is evident that these direct quotes are not identical in their wording nor do they convey exactly the same idea. When asked whether He is the Son of God, Matthew quotes Christ as saying, "Thou hast said," in other words, "You have said it." Mark has the Savior giving a direct affirmative, "I am." Luke records the Lord initially avoiding a direct response to the inquiry by stating, "If I tell you, ye will not believe." According to Luke, they then ask Him again, "Art thou then the Son of God" (Luke 22:70), to which the Savior replies, "Ye say that I am." Either the Savior answered this question directly or He did not. These gospel passages obviously disagree as to what exactly the Lord did say.

As for the second part of Christ's response, Matthew and Mark record the Lord as saying that He will return "coming in the clouds of heaven," while Luke completely omits this phrase from his version. It appears that textual changes have been made by careless scribes since the original transmission was given.

Obviously, these passages do not detract from the overall spirit of the gospel message, nor do they deal with major doctrinal issues. Nevertheless, they do serve to illustrate that those who insist on complete biblical inerrancy stand on shaky ground. A few more examples will reveal that some errors are substantial enough to influence modern Christian beliefs and practices.

In Exodus 32:14, we read, "And the *Lord repented* of the evil which he thought to do unto his people." Is the Lord capable of thinking of an evil act, much less committing one? Does the Lord have need of repentance? As he was inspired by the Holy Ghost, Joseph Smith received a more correct reading of this particular scripture, "And the Lord said unto Moses, *If they [children of Israel] will repent of the evil which they have done,* I will spare them, and turn away my fierce wrath; but, behold, thou shalt execute judgment upon all that will not repent of this evil this day. Therefore, see thou do this thing that I have commanded thee, or I will execute all that which I had thought to do unto my people."[42]

The Old Testament prophet, Amos, poses the question, "Shall there be evil in a city, and the Lord hath not *done* it?" (Amos 3:6). The translators of the Revised Standard Version render the same passage to read, "Does evil befall a city, unless the Lord has *done* it?" Surely the righteous Lord is not the perpetrator of any evil activity. Guided by the Spirit of revelation, Joseph Smith restored this passage to its original wording and meaning: "Shall there be evil in a city, and the Lord hath not *known* it?"[43]

In a letter to the Corinthians, the apostle Paul writes that "it is a shame for women to *speak* in the church" (1 Corinthians 14:35). How many modern churches observe this scriptural teaching? The Spirit revealed to Joseph Smith that this passage more accurately reads that women should not "rule" in the church,[44] meaning women enjoy the same privileges as men of participating in worship services while priesthood leadership is reserved for worthy males.

The Apostle John wrote, *"No man hath seen God at any time;* the only begotten Son, which is in the bosom of the Father, he hath declared him" (John 1:18). This contradicts Moses's firsthand encounter with the Lord: "And the Lord spake unto Moses face to face, as a man speaketh unto his friend" (Exodus 33:11). On another occasion, Moses and others "saw the God of Israel" (Exodus 24:10). Again, the Lord has provided further light on this matter through the instrumentality of Joseph Smith. This passage originally read, "And no man hath seen God at any time, *except he hath borne record of the Son; for except it is through him no man can be saved."*[45] Only worthy witnesses, such as the prophets, who have testified of the divinity of the Savior, have seen God.

Related to this same topic, the Lord said to Moses, "Thou canst not see my face: for there shall no man see me, and live" (Exodus 33:20). The Bible actually records many different occasions wherein prophets, Moses included, have seen God and lived. Under the guidance of the Spirit, Joseph Smith restored this passage to its original reading: "And he said unto Moses, Thou canst not see my face *at this time,* lest mine anger be kindled against thee also, and I destroy thee, and thy people; for there shall no man among them see me at this time, and live, for they are exceeding sinful. And no *sinful man* hath at any time, neither shall there be any *sinful man* at any time, that shall see my face and live."[46] While the worthy and faithful may see God and endure His presence, the wicked are not eligible for such a glorious blessing.

In one of the greatest Old Testament stories, Moses sought Israel's release from Egyptian servitude, "but the *Lord hardened Pharaoh's heart*, and he would not let them go" (Exodus 10:27). Would the Lord compel someone to harden their heart? Would God cause someone to sin? The Joseph Smith translation reads, "But *Pharaoh hardened his heart*, and he would not let them go."[47]

In the Old Testament story of the anointing of David as king over Israel by Samuel, the biblical record reads, "But the Spirit of the Lord departed from Saul, and *an evil spirit from the Lord* troubled him. And Saul's servants said unto him, Behold now, *an evil spirit from God* troubleth thee" (1 Samuel 16:14-15). The notion that God sends evil spirits to anyone is false, for "all things which are good cometh of God; and that which is evil cometh of the devil" (Moroni 7:12). Joseph Smith corrected this mistranslation to read: "But the Spirit of the Lord departed from Saul, and *an evil spirit which was not of the Lord* troubled him. And Saul's servants said unto him, Behold now, an evil spirit which is not of God troubleth thee."[48]

There are virtually thousands of biblical passages that have been clarified or expanded through the efforts of Joseph Smith as he served as an instrument in the hands of the Lord to restore these ancient records to their original condition. The biblical additions, restorations, corrections, and clarifications made by this latter-day prophet of God are quite substantial and would serve as enlightening reading for any serious student of the Bible. In the capacity of prophet of the Most High God, Joseph Smith revised 3,410 verses of the Bible. In the Book of Genesis alone, the Prophet made changes in approximately 50% of the verses and added the equivalent of 250 new verses, while in Matthew he made changes to 58% of its 1,071 verses.[49]

Many may consider it blasphemy for someone to change the text of the Bible, but isn't that what occurs every time a new translation of the Bible is published by a translating committee? Compare any two biblical translations to discover the diversity between the texts. For example, in one of Paul's letters to the Corinthians, the King James translators record the following passage: "Let no man seek his own, but every man another's *wealth*" (1 Corinthians 10:24). The Revised Standard Version translators record this verse as follows: "Let no one seek his own *good*, but the *good* of his neighbor." The New International Version reads: "Nobody should seek his own good, but the *good* of others."

It is evident that the changes made in the wording by the various biblical translating committees can alter the actual meaning of the texts, as this example illustrates. Obviously, there is a difference between seeking another's "wealth" and another's "good."

Joseph Smith received inspiration from God to render this passage as follows: "Let not man seek therefore his own, but every man another's *good*."[50] It is interesting to note that he made his revision by 1833 without the aid of more recent manuscript discoveries which have facilitated the work of modern translating committees. Archaeological developments in the field of ancient religious writings have served to vindicate Joseph Smith's sacred calling as a prophet of God.

A previously mentioned passage will serve well as another example of divergence in meaning among the different versions of the Bible. According to the King James translators, Moses quoted the Lord as saying, "And I will harden Pharoah's heart, and multiply my signs and my wonders in the land of Egypt. But Pharoah shall not hearken unto you" (Exodus 7:3-4). The New International Version reads similarly: "But I will harden Pharoah's heart, and though I multiply my miraculous signs and wonders in Egypt, he will not listen to you."

Two other translations of the same passage indicate that the Lord did not harden Pharoah's heart, but rather allowed Pharoah to harden his own heart. A Translation of the Old Testament Scriptures From the Original Hebrew by Helen Spurrell translates this passage to read, "And I will allow Pharoah's heart to harden..." The Emphasized Bible: A New Translation by J.B. Rotherham reads, "But I will suffer [allow or permit] Pharoah to harden his heart..." These last two versions agree with Joseph Smith's 1833 translation which reads, "And Pharoah will harden his heart..." As in the previous example, the different biblical versions offer different readings which convey different meanings.

These, and thousands of other translation variations, indicate that diversity in meaning as well as wording exists among the many versions of the Bible available today. As these well-intentioned translating committees attempt to produce the most accurate version of the Bible possible, they are indeed changing the text.

In fact, over 100,000 changes have been made from the time of the King James Version down to the Revised Standard Version in an effort to produce the most correct rendition possible of these sacred writings.[51] Of all the available translations, who can say which translation is the best, or as some assert, which is perfect? For that matter, which of the thousands of varying ancient manuscripts represents the correct transmission of God's word?

This very act of constant revision by translating committees is witness to the fact that the Bible, in its present condition, is not perfect, otherwise why attempt to change or improve it? And what of the Prophet Joseph Smith's effort to improve the Bible? The Latter-day Saints believe that a biblical translation produced by a chosen prophet of God as guided by the Holy Ghost is much more reliable than one produced by a committee of individuals guided by their own collective human intellect and majority opinions. If passages have been removed from the original manuscripts which are no longer accessible to man, the committees will never know it, whereas a prophet of God can receive the revelation anew.

Joseph Smith spoke for all sincere students of the Bible when he said, "I believe the Bible as it read when it came from the pen of the original writers. Ignorant translators, careless transcribers, or designing and corrupt priests have committed many errors."[52] The evidence revealed in the ancient manuscripts and more recent archaeological discoveries clearly corroborates this statement. Although we do not possess any of the original biblical manuscripts, modern revelation from God does give us some indication of the damage done by the careless and corrupt keepers of these sacred writings.

God's Commentary on the Bible

The corruption of the prophetic Jewish records which constitute our modern Bible was foreseen by an ancient American prophet almost 600 years before Christ: "The book [Holy Bible] that thou beholdest is a record of the Jews, which contains the covenants of the Lord, which he hath made unto the house of Israel; and it also containeth many of the prophecies of the holy prophets...

"...When it proceeded forth from the mouth of a Jew it contained the fulness of the gospel of the Lord, of whom the twelve apostles bear record; and they bear record according to the truth which is in the Lamb of God.

"Wherefore, these things go forth from the Jews in purity unto the Gentiles, according to the truth which is in God.

"And after they go forth by the hand of the twelve apostles of the Lamb, from the Jews unto the Gentiles, thou seest the formation of that great and abominable church, which is most abominable above all other churches; for behold, *they [corrupt men] have taken away from the gospel of the Lamb many parts which are plain and most precious;* and also many covenants of the Lord have they taken away.

"And all this have they done that they might pervert the right ways of the Lord, that they might blind the eyes and harden the hearts of the children of men.

"Wherefore, thou seest that after the book [Bible] hath gone forth through the hands of the great and abominable church, that *there are many plain and precious things taken away from the book, which is the book of the Lamb of God.*

"And after these plain and precious things were taken away it goeth forth unto all the nations of the Gentiles; and after it goeth forth unto all the nations of the Gentiles, yea, even across the many waters which thou hast seen with the Gentiles which have gone forth out of captivity, thou seest — *because of the many plain and precious things which have been taken out of the book,* which were plain unto the understanding of the children of men, according to the plainness which is in the Lamb of God — *because of these things which are taken away out of the gospel of the Lamb, an exceedingly great many do stumble"* (The Book of Mormon, 1 Nephi 13:23-29). Recent discoveries of ancient texts stand as powerful witnesses to the veracity and divinity of this prophetic utterance.

THE SCRIPTURES AND THE CHURCH

Possession of the Bible alone is not adequate to establish Christ's Church. The Bible is a product of the Church; the Church is not a product of the Bible. The apostles were not guided solely by the scriptures as they directed the operations of the Savior's Church. They were guided by direct revelation from God, Peter's vision instructing him to teach the gospel to the Gentiles being just one of many examples (Acts 10). The apostles did not have a New Testament to determine their actions or teachings, for their very acts and teachings created the New Testament.

Consider the issue of circumcision. If the apostles were to receive their instruction from the scriptural record that existed in their day, namely, the Old Testament writings, then they would have had to require circumcision for all new male converts of the Church.[53] However, modern revelation was their guide, not ancient scriptures. The Jews during the time of Christ made the mistake of believing that the scriptures replaced the living oracles of God. They read the scriptures daily in their synagogues, while persecuting the living prophets who attempted to give them further revelation and instruction from God.

In short, the true and living Church, the one guided by a living God who reveals His will through direct revelation, is not guided solely by scripture, although the scriptures play a vital role in the daily lives of church members. The true Church actually creates new scripture by virtue of its actions, priesthood authority, and continuing revelations from God. In the Savior's Church, this has always been the pattern in the past and will continue to be the procedure in the future, for God is "the same yesterday, and today, and forever" (Hebrews 13:8).

MISUNDERSTOOD TEACHINGS CONCERNING THE BIBLE

Many believe that the Bible is complete, providing us with all that is necessary for our salvation. There are a few scriptures which are typically quoted in support of this argument: "According as his divine power hath *given unto us all things* that pertain unto life and godliness" (2 Peter 1:3). "Henceforth I call you not servants; for the servant knoweth not what his lord doeth: but I have called you friends; for *all things that I have heard of my Father I have made known unto you*" (John 15:15).

It is one thing to claim that the ancient apostles possessed all gospel knowledge that the Father conveyed to Christ, and quite another to claim that all such knowledge is still recorded and preserved in our present-day Bible. Much in the way of divine instruction and revelation was never committed to writing. As for those inspired utterances which were recorded, after the death of the apostles, wicked and uninspired men removed many "plain and precious" passages from the biblical books. This is currently being substantiated by recent archaeological discoveries like the Dead Sea Scrolls.

As further scriptural support to advance the idea that the Bible is the only word of God, Revelation 22:18-19 is probably the most commonly quoted passage: "For I testify unto every man that heareth the words of the prophecy of this book, If any man shall add unto these things, God shall add unto him the plagues that are written in this book: And if any man shall take away from the words of the book of this prophecy, God shall take away his part out of the book of life, and out of the holy city, and from the things which are written in this book." Since it appears in the last chapter of the last book of the Bible, that is, the Book of Revelation, this warning is often incorrectly applied to the entire Bible when in reality John was referring only to the Book of Revelation.

In order to more clearly understand this scripture, several

enlightening observations should be made. First, the same John that recorded this scripture (Revelation 22:18-19), also wrote the First, Second, and Third Epistle of John at later dates. If Revelation 22:18-19 does indeed instruct man not to add to the Bible, then John would have been violating the very command that he himself recorded by writing these later epistles.

Second, the Bible did not exist in its current form at the time John recorded this scripture, nor did the biblical authors give any indication that they knew their writings would be later compiled together to form one volume of scripture. John wrote Revelation around A.D.95,[54] while the entire Bible did not appear in its current form until the early part of the 17th century.

Third, Moses made a similar statement, warning, "Ye shall not add unto the word which I command you, neither shall ye diminish ought from it" (Deuteronomy 4:2). If we interpret this in the same way that many today interpret Revelation 22:18-19, then we must reject everything from Deuteronomy to Revelation.

Fourth, perhaps the strongest argument lies in a closer reading of John's warning. He clearly indicates that no "*man* shall add unto these things." This in no way restricts Almighty God from adding to His own revealed word as He sees fit in His infinite wisdom. Who would dare to attempt to close God's mouth as He poured out further truth from the heavens? And as history bears witness, God always reveals His will through faithful men chosen to be holy prophets.

THE LATTER-DAY SAINTS AND THE BIBLE

It is not the purpose of this discussion to trivialize or degrade the Bible in any way. Latter-day Saints regard the Bible as holy scripture, as it constitutes a vital part of the LDS Church's canonized standard works. Latter-day Saints love the Bible and hold it in high esteem as they study its pages and try to live the eternal gospel principles found therein. In fact, on October 15, 1982, The Church of Jesus Christ of Latter-day Saints received an award from the Layman's National Bible Committee for its own edition of the King James Bible. The citation reads: "Presented to The Church of Jesus Christ of Latter-day Saints. In appreciation of outstanding service to the Bible cause through the publication of its own new edition of the King James Version which features interpretive chapter headings, a simplified footnote system and the linking of references to all other LDS scriptures — thereby greatly enhancing the study of the Bible by its membership."[55]

While Latter-day Saints believe this holy record contains the revelations from God as they were conveyed to ancient prophets of the Old World, they also understand that thousands of years of time and generations of uninspired men have led to some alterations of the text. To think that man has perfectly preserved these writings over the centuries while concurrently committing all sorts of atrocities against his fellowman in the name of religion is to ignore some critical historical facts.

Personally, my faith is in God, not the Bible nor man's ability to preserve the Bible. I love the Bible for what it is — a sacred volume of scripture. However, I realize that man has tampered with the original text. This does not diminish my faith in God nor the value I place in the Bible, for I also realize that God has provided additional scriptures and latter-day prophets which serve to shed light on biblical teachings. Actually, I find it quite amazing how well the sacred writings comprising our modern-day Bible have survived centuries of spiritual darkness.

GOD'S WORD IS UNENDING

The Latter-day Saints believe that the Bible is the word of God and that it contains important eternal truths, yet they do not limit God's wisdom to this one volume of scripture. We believe "every word that proceedeth out of the mouth of God" (Matthew 4:4). He has revealed many great truths in the past, and likewise, He will reveal many more great and glorious truths to those who have ears to hear.

The Bible is one part of a greater whole of gospel truth. As Latter-day Saints, we pray that the people of the world will open their eyes and hearts to the additional light and knowledge that is available to them if they are only willing to receive it. We invite people of all nations to hold on to everything they have which is good and true, then add to it that which our Heavenly Father has revealed, and will continue to reveal, through His prophets in these last days. There is so much more to learn of the grand universe in which we live. We know so little of the creation of the heavens and earth, of the resurrection and judgment yet to come, of life in God's glorious kingdom, or of a thousand other equally fascinating and important truths. God has much more to reveal in His own due time according to His infinite wisdom, for He will teach us "precept upon precept; line upon line, line upon line; here a little, and there a little" (Isaiah 28:10).

God's work is to bring to pass the immortality and eternal life of His children (Moses 1:39), consequently His work is far from complete. As long as there are men and women on earth striving to return to their Eternal Father, there will be a need for continuing revelation.

7

THE BOOK OF MORMON

THE first time someone gave me a copy of the Book of Mormon, I was so unimpressed with its appearance that I put it on a bookshelf where I would soon forget about it. Most of what I had heard regarding this book and the Church which distributed it was quite negative, therefore I saw little reason to open its cover. How simple it seemed to discount any value this book might have to offer merely on the merits of hearsay, peer pressure, false tradition, and preconceived notions. In a sense, I allowed others to do my thinking for me.

The next time I encountered this book of scripture, which was at least a year later, it changed my life forever. The LDS missionaries that I met at my brother's house encouraged me to dust off my old copy and challenged me to read it and inquire of God as to its truthfulness. By now, the Spirit of the Lord had sufficiently softened my hard heart and stiff neck enough to convince me that this intriguing book deserved another look.

As I stated earlier, it was while reading the Book of Mormon that the Holy Ghost witnessed to me that the gospel of Jesus Christ had been restored in its fullness to the earth by way of heavenly messengers. The Spirit of the Lord testified to my spirit that the Book of Mormon was the word of God as plainly as if God Almighty Himself appeared to me personally to convey this simple truth. Others may attempt to assault my convictions, however I cannot deny what God has chosen to reveal. The most startling outcome of my newfound spiritual testimony is the the profound impact it has had on my entire way of thinking. My perception of self, my life, and the world in which I live has totally changed — and I believe for the better. Previously subscribing to a philosophy made up of moral relativism and situational ethics, I now know the universe is governed by eternal laws and absolute truths.

Not only has the Book of Mormon completely changed my life, but I have seen it change the lives of others as well. At the time that I joined the LDS Church, I was single and living with a friend who had recently gone through a divorce. This young man and I were both in our young 20's and had known each other since our earliest days together in kindergarten. One could hardly ask for a more loyal and dedicated friend — we truly felt like brothers.

Our close friendship, nevertheless, became threatened by my sudden lifestyle change. My friends thought my judgment must have been truly impaired when I joined the Mormon Church. My roommate was especially aware that there was something dramatically different about me, but he couldn't quite put his finger on it. He didn't say much about it, but I knew he was watching me closely to see where all of this was heading.

Over the next several months, he began to meet many of my newfound friends from Church, most of whom were full-time missionaries and young, single adults. I could tell he was impressed by their friendliness and sincere interest in him. It wasn't long before he began to attend Church socials with me, allowing him to meet an even wider circle of Church members. He soon began to ask himself what it was that made these good people so happy about life and so desirous to follow the Savior. It became obvious that he wanted to experience the blessings of joy and brotherhood that he saw me enjoying.

He decided to accept the challenge to talk with the missionaries in order to learn more about the LDS Church and its teachings. As he studied the Book of Mormon and prayed to God for guidance, I witnessed a wonderful change take place in my good friend. His speech, his behavior, his goals, his desires, virtually everything about him, seemed to elevate to a higher level as the Spirit of God wrought a mighty change in his heart. He had become a new creature in Christ. My joy was great as I heard him bear solemn and powerful testimony that the Book of Mormon was true.

Just as it had done for me and millions of other truth-seekers throughout the world, the Book of Mormon changed my friend's life. Within weeks, I baptized him a member of the Lord's Church. Eventually, he met a beautiful young lady in the Church whom he could take to the Lord's temple, making sacred covenants and sealing their love and their lives together for time and all eternity. My lifelong friend has tasted the good fruit of the gospel by availing himself of the eternal truths found in the Book of Mormon. Today he finds great joy in knowing that his relationship with God and his understanding of the purpose of life has grown due to this sacred book of scripture.

I have seen the powerful impact that this book has had on the lives of myself and others. I have seen it make grown people cry with tears of joy while reading from its pages, as it did for an agnostic woman I taught as a missionary in France. I have seen it settle disputes over doctrine among those of differing faiths. I have seen it captivate my inquisitive children as we conduct family scripture study within our home. The Lord has given us the Book of Mormon in these last days to gather His scattered children from the four corners of the world in order that He can touch our hearts and change our lives forever.

THE STICK OF JOSEPH

The Old Testament prophet Ezekiel was aware of an inspired record which would come forth and would be distinct from the biblical record when he wrote, "The word of the Lord came again unto me, saying, Moreover, thou son of man, take thee one stick, and write upon it, For Judah, and for the children of Israel his companions: then take another stick, and write upon it, For Joseph, the stick of Ephraim, and for all the house of Israel his companions: And join them one to another into one stick; and they shall become one in thine hand.

"And when the children of thy people shall speak unto thee, saying, Wilt thou not shew us what thou meanest by these? Say unto them, Thus saith the Lord God; Behold I will take the *stick of Joseph,* which is in the hand of Ephraim, and the tribes of Israel his fellows, and will put them with him, even with the *stick of Judah,* and make them one stick, and they shall be one in mine hand" (Ezekiel 37:15-19).

The stick of Judah is the Holy Bible. Recent archaeological discoveries confirm that a "stick," or "wood," in Hebrew, refers to a writing tablet consisting of wood and wax which was commonly used in Babylon during Ezekiel's time.[1] In fact, these recent findings have spawned more enlightened translations of this scripture found in Ezekiel. The New English Bible reads as follows: "These were the words of the Lord to me: Man, take *one leaf of a wooden tablet* and write on it, 'Judah and his associates of Israel.' Then take another leaf and write on it, 'Joseph, the leaf of Ephraim and all of his associates of Israel.' Now *bring the two together to form one tablet; then they will be a folding tablet* in your hand. These are the words of the Lord God: I am taking the leaf of Joseph, which belongs to Ephraim and his associate tribes of Israel, and joining it to the leaf of Judah. Thus I shall make them one tablet." The Bible, the stick or leaf, of Judah, was written primarily by Jewish prophets as they recorded God's dealings with the people of Judah. It is the word of God.

If the Bible is the stick, or leaf, of Judah, what is the stick of Joseph and who has come forth with it? The stick of Joseph is the Book of

Mormon. As previously mentioned, it is a record of God's dealings with the tribe of Joseph as it was recorded by prophets of God who were descendants of the same Joseph who was sold into Egypt by his brothers. It, too, is the word of God. The Book of Mormon does not supplant the Bible; these two records complement each other, for as the Lord said, "they shall be one in mine hand" (Ezekiel 37:19). In other words, these two holy records would both bear witness that God lives and that Jesus is the Christ, the Savior of the world.

The Book of Mormon is, as its subtitle declares, "another testament of Jesus Christ." This book of scripture fulfills the ancient law of witnesses which demands that "in the mouth of two or three witnesses shall every word be established" (2 Corinthians 13:1; Deuteronomy 17:6; Matthew 18:16).

THE DIVINE ORIGINS OF THE BOOK OF MORMON

Around 600 B.C., the Lord led a Hebrew prophet named Lehi — a descendant of the Old Testament prophet, Joseph — and his family, away from Jerusalem just prior to the Babylonian captivity. Lehi's family, along with another family, was safely guided to the western hemisphere to land somewhere on the western coast of South America. There they multiplied and prospered and eventually became a great nation. The Book of Mormon records the rise and fall of this great civilization that prospered when it heeded the word of God and declined when it fell into spiritual darkness.

Just as prophets in the Old World received revelations and recorded them, so, too, did prophets in the New World. Not possessing the high-tech communication networks that span the globe today, the inhabitants of the American continents were unable to receive direction from the prophets living in the region of Jerusalem. Therefore, God in His infinite wisdom chose certain righteous men from among those who lived in the New World to be prophets, thereby according His children there the same divine guidance that He offered those who inhabited the Old World.

The writings of these ancient American prophets were handed down from generation to generation until they were eventually compiled and abridged into one volume of scripture around A.D. 400 by Mormon, one of the last in this long line of prophets. This volume of holy scripture, most of which spans the millennium from 600 B.C. to A.D. 400, bears the name of he who compiled and abridged it, thus, it is called the Book of Mormon.

Mormon gave this scriptural record, which was fashioned on thin, hammered plates of gold, to his son, Moroni, who in turn added further scripture as inspired by the Holy Ghost before finally burying the plates in a stone box for safe keeping. Moroni was the last prophet to contribute to this ancient record, for his people were nearly annihilated by the ravages of ongoing wars fueled by their own wickedness and lust for blood.

Over 1,400 years later, in the year 1827, Moroni, by then a resurrected being, was commissioned by God to deliver these sacred writings to a young man named Joseph Smith, who had been prepared by the Lord to receive them. By the power of God, Joseph Smith translated a portion of these ancient writings from reformed Egyptian into English in order that they might serve as a witness to the divinity of Jesus Christ and the restoration of His gospel on earth. Now available in over 80 languages, the Book of Mormon has truly come forth to be one in God's hand with the Holy Bible, just as Ezekiel prophesied long ago.

THE MESSAGE OF THE BOOK OF MORMON

Perhaps the greatest event recorded in the Book of Mormon is the Savior's visit to the inhabitants of ancient America. Subsequent to His resurrection, Christ told His disciples in Jerusalem, "And other sheep I have, which are not of this fold: them also I must bring, and they shall hear my voice; and there shall be one fold, and one shepherd" (John 10:16). Christ was speaking of His disciples in ancient America who were also awaiting His atoning sacrifice and resurrection. Is not Christ the Savior of all mankind?

The Book of Mormon records the glorious appearance of the resurrected Savior to His disciples in ancient America. It records many of the beautiful gospel truths that He taught them. It records His appointment of twelve special witnesses to lead and guide His Church in the New World. It preserves for all to read the magnificent prayer that He offered to the Father in His disciples' behalf. It describes in incredible detail the wondrous signs witnessed by all those in America at the time of the Savior's birth in Bethlehem, as well as the great cataclysmic upheavals and destruction that occurred when He was crucified on Golgotha.

It discusses in great beauty and simplicity such gospel principles as the resurrection of the dead, the purpose of life, repentance, baptism, the final judgment, eternal salvation, and the destination of man's spirit after mortal death. Most importantly, it serves as a second witness to the world that Jesus Christ is the Son of God and the Savior of the world. What honest truth-seeking Christian would deny him or herself the opportunity to read these inspiring and enlightening passages brought forth by the hand of the almighty God in these last days?

Testing the Book of Mormon

The Latter-day Saints invite people of all races, creeds, nations, and tongues to read the Book of Mormon and learn for themselves of its divine authenticity. Solomon once claimed that to judge a matter before hearing it was not wise (Proverbs 18:13). The Apostle Paul wrote, "Prove [or test] all things; hold fast that which is good" (1 Thessalonians 5:21). Who can honestly say whether the Book of Mormon has divine origins without investigating its contents firsthand?

An honest perusal of the Book of Mormon will reveal that no man (or group of men), much less an unlearned man such as Joseph Smith, could have written this profound and internally consistent volume of scripture without divine assistance. God is its author. For those who claim otherwise, the challenge is open to them to duplicate the feat.

Many nonmembers incorrectly suppose that the Latter-day Saints' acceptance of additional scripture, such as the Book of Mormon, necessarily implies their rejection of the Bible. Modern-day scripture and revelation tends to augment, not diminish, Latter-day Saints' reverence and understanding of the Bible. Just as the Jews were not expected to reject the Old Testament in order to accept and believe the additional enlightenment provided by the New Testament, people today are not expected to reject the ancient writings comprising our modern Bible in order to receive the further light and knowledge offered by additional scripture and revelation.[2]

The Lord makes a solemn promise to all those who will read the Book of Mormon with an open heart and sincere desire to know the truth. "And when ye shall receive these things [meaning the things written in the Book of Mormon], I would exhort you that ye would ask God, the Eternal Father, in the name of Christ, if these things are not true; and if ye shall ask with a sincere heart, with real intent, having faith in Christ, he will manifest the truth of it unto you, by the power of the Holy Ghost" (The Book of Mormon, Moroni 10:4).

Anyone who will read the Book of Mormon, with an open mind, that is, free of any preconceived biases or beliefs, ponder its contents, and then seek divine assistance through humble prayer to determine its origin, will surely learn of its truthfulness. Admittedly, this requires a great amount of humility, for one must consign himself to the fact that he does not know the truth and is prepared to submit to the Lord's Spirit for guidance and truth. I honestly believe that if one feels foolish for reading the Book of Mormon and testing the Lord's promise, or if one reads it with the intent of finding fault, then God's requirements for obtaining a spiritual testimony are not met and the truth will not be manifested to them by the Spirit of God. I personally know that the Book of Mormon is the word of God, for it has been revealed to me by the power of the Holy Ghost.

This is the invitation offered by the prophets of this latter-day dispensation, found in the introduction to the Book of Mormon:"We invite all men everywhere to read the Book of Mormon, to ponder in their hearts the message it contains, and then to ask God, the Eternal Father, in the name of Christ if the book is true. Those who pursue this course and ask in faith will gain a testimony of its truth and divinity by the power of the Holy Ghost.

"Those who gain this divine witness from the Holy Spirit will also come to know by the same power that Jesus Christ is the Savior of the world, that Joseph Smith is His revelator and prophet in these last days, and that The Church of Jesus Christ of Latter-day Saints is the Lord's kingdom once again established on the earth, preparatory to the second coming of the Messiah."

ACQUIRING A SPIRITUAL TESTIMONY OF THE TRUTH

I have heard it said that a person cannot learn the truth by kneeling before God in prayer, or that a person cannot trust his or her own feelings. However, in His Sermon on the Mount, the Savior taught, "Ask, and it shall be given you; seek, and ye shall find; knock, and it shall be opened unto you" (Matthew 7:7). On this same matter, the Apostle James wrote, "If any of you lack wisdom, let him ask of God, that giveth to all men liberally, and upbraideth [criticize or scold] not; and it shall be given him" (James 1:5). What could be more important than asking our Heavenly Father to teach us truth and the way to salvation? If we ask in faith, He has promised to give it to us. And how shall it be given or taught to us? The Savior answers, "But the Comforter, which is the *Holy Ghost*, whom the Father will send in my name, *he shall teach you all things*, and bring all things to your remembrance, whatsoever I have said unto you" (John 14:26). "Howbeit when he, the Spirit of truth, is come, he will guide you into all truth" (John 16:13). The Spirit of truth, the Holy Ghost, will teach us the truth of all things.

Perhaps the greatest truth we can learn while in this life is the teaching that Jesus Christ is the Son of God and the Savior of the world. In his epistle to the saints at Corinth, the apostle Paul explained how this truth is acquired. "Wherefore I give you to understand, that no man speaking by the Spirit of God calleth Jesus accursed: and that *no man can say that Jesus is the Lord, but by the Holy Ghost"* (1 Corinthians 12:3). There is only one way to gain a real and lasting testimony of the truth that Jesus is the Christ, the Messiah, come to save all mankind from the Fall. That truth must be distilled upon the spirit of man by the power of the Holy Spirit of God. Spirit must witness to spirit.

Paul taught that the gospel must be preached by the power of the Spirit to be understood: "And my speech and my preaching was not with enticing words of man's wisdom, but in demonstration of the Spirit and of power:

"That your faith should not stand in the wisdom of men, but in the power of God.

"Now we have received, not the spirit of the world, but the spirit which is of God; that we might know the things that are freely given to us of God.

"Which things also we speak, not in the words which man's wisdom teacheth; but which *the Holy Ghost teacheth;* comparing spiritual things with spiritual.

"But *the natural man receiveth not the things of the Spirit of God: for they are foolishness unto him: neither can he know them, because they are spiritually discerned"* (1 Corinthians 2:4-5, 12-14).

Whether truth is sought through preaching, scripture study, or prayer, the power of the Holy Ghost must be the ultimate channel by which truth is conveyed to the truthseeker. A perfect illustration of how truth or the Lord's will can be ascertained through prayer is found in the ancient apostles' efforts to determine an apostolic replacement for their fallen colleague, Judas. "And they prayed, and said, Thou, Lord, which knowest the hearts of all men, shew whether of these two thou hast chosen" (Acts 1:24). By the mode of communication which the Lord has established for us to commune with Him during mortality, namely, prayer, the ancient apostles were able to learn the will of God concerning the choice for a new apostle. Likewise, we can approach our Father in humble prayer, asking Him to guide us in our quest for truth and knowledge. We can be assured He will hear and honor our humble request, teaching us the truth of all things by the power of the Holy Spirit.

As for the assertion that we cannot trust the feelings of our heart or the whisperings of the still, small voice of the Spirit to our minds, the experience of the two disciples of Christ on the road to Emmaus after the Savior's resurrection provides an adequate response. The risen Lord accompanied these two unsuspecting disciples during their journey, expounding the scriptures and relating them to recent events of their day. The resurrected Lord stood before them, walked with them, taught them, and ate with them, yet they did not recognize Him. It was not until His departure that "they said one to another, *Did not our heart burn within us,* while he talked with us by the way, and while he opened to us the scriptures?" (Luke 24:32).

The Savior personally preached and quoted scripture to them, but it was the burning of their hearts caused by the Holy Ghost (what Latter-day Saints often refer to as the "burning of the bosom") that brought them to the realization that they had witnessed their resurrected Savior and had heard the truth as it flowed from His lips. They had heard the truth and they knew it, for the Spirit of God bore witness to their spirits, that is, to their hearts.

The day of Pentecost serves as another illustration of the spiritual witness that touches the hearts of truthseekers. When the apostles of Christ gathered together on this day, "they were all filled with the Holy Ghost" (Acts 2:4), as the Apostle Peter stood up to preach the gospel of Jesus Christ to all those assembled. As Peter's great sermon on the mission of the Savior came to a close, "they were *pricked in their heart*" (Acts 2:37).

It is this same pricking or burning of the heart that millions of sincere readers of the Book of Mormon have received as they approached their Heavenly Father in prayer with "real intent" to know the truthfulness of this sacred volume of scripture. All the flowery argumentation of the world and the philosophical reasoning of mankind cannot replace or restrain the burning witness of the Holy Spirit of God that touches the heart and inspires the mind of man.

When Latter-day Saints make reference to their personal testimony of the gospel of Jesus Christ, it is important to understand that it is not founded upon mere human feelings or emotions. Rather, a testimony is conveyed to the profoundest depths of man's soul by the power of the Holy Spirit of God. When Almighty God communicates eternal truths to the spirit of man, pure intelligence flows from Deity to mortal.

In response to a humble and prayerful inquiry, Oliver Cowdery, a scribe to the Prophet Joseph Smith, received the following reply from the Lord, "Behold, thou knowest that thou hast inquired of me and I did enlighten thy mind; and now I tell thee these things that thou mayest know that thou hast been enlightened by the Spirit of truth" (Doctrine & Covenants 6:15). On another occasion, the Lord informed Oliver, "Yea, behold, I will tell you in your mind and in your heart, by the Holy Ghost, which shall come upon you and which shall dwell in your heart. Now, behold, this is the spirit of revelation" (Doctrine & Covenants 8:2). Each of us may obtain spiritual guidance and enlightenment, just as Oliver Cowdery did on this occasion. While it might be true that we cannot always trust our human emotions or feelings, we can always trust the Spirit of the Lord as it enlightens our mind and touches our heart, thereby causing the mind and will of God to permeate our very being and eternal truths to be spiritually understood.

One young man once told me that he prayed about the Book of Mormon and did not receive a spiritual witness that it was true. He concluded that the book must not be true and refused to give God's promise a second try. After further discussion, he hinted that he felt foolish for even praying about the book. He also revealed that he clung tightly to his preconceived beliefs while approaching the Lord in prayer. In so doing, he violated two preconditions of God's promise to grant the witness that comes by the power of the Holy Ghost. First, his feelings of foolishness in asking his Heavenly Father about the truthfulness of a particular matter demonstrated that he did not ask with "a sincere heart."

Secondly, by holding on to his old beliefs, he did not approach the Lord with an open mind. In shutting his heart and mind to new personal revelation from the Lord, he perhaps showed a lack of "real intent." He also demonstrated lack of perseverance and resolve by asking only once. The Lord will test our faith and desire to know the truth by granting an answer to our prayers on His own terms and according to His own timetable.

God's Commentary on Continuous Revelation

For those who dismiss the divine origins of the Book of Mormon, insisting that the Bible is the only word of God at man's disposal, God offers a powerful rejoinder: "Wo be unto him that shall say: We have received the word of God, and we need no more of the word of God, for we have enough!

"For behold, thus saith the Lord God: I will give unto the children of men line upon line, precept upon precept, here a little and there a little; and blessed are those who hearken unto my precepts, and lend an ear unto my counsel, for they shall learn wisdom; for unto him that receiveth I will give more; and from them that shall say, We have enough, from them shall be taken away even that which they have.

"Thou fool, that shall say: A Bible, we have got a Bible, and we need no more Bible. Have ye obtained a Bible save it were by the Jews?

"Know ye not that there are more nations than one? Know ye not that I, the Lord your God, have created all men, and that I remember those who are upon the isles of the sea; and that I rule in the heavens above and in the earth beneath; and I bring forth my word unto the children of men, yea, even upon all the nations of the earth?

"*Wherefore murmur ye, because that ye shall receive more of my word?* Know ye not that the testimony of two nations is a witness unto you that I am God, that I remember one nation like unto another? Wherefore, I speak the same words unto one nation like unto another. And when the two nations shall run together the testimony of the two nations shall run together also.

"And I do this that I may prove unto many that I am the same yesterday, today, and forever; and that I speak forth my words according to mine own pleasure. And *because that I have spoken one word ye need not suppose that I cannot speak another; for my work is not yet finished;* neither shall it be until the end of man, neither from that time henceforth and forever.

"*Wherefore, because that ye have a Bible ye need not suppose that it contains all my words; neither need ye suppose that I have not caused more to be written*" (The Book of Mormon, 2 Nephi 28:29-30; 29:6-10).

8

THE DOCTRINE OF ETERNAL FAMILIES

THROUGH His prophets, the Lord has taught us that marriage between a man and woman is a holy institution that has been provided for the benefit of all mankind. After placing Adam in the Garden of Eden, He declared, "It is not good that the man should be alone" (Genesis 2:18). The Lord then provided a mate for Adam and instructed him to "cleave unto his wife," Eve, in order that they might become one flesh, and that they might "be fruitful, and multiply, and replenish the earth" (Genesis 2:24; 1:28). The Apostle Paul taught that "marriage is honourable in all" (Hebrews 13:4), and that "neither is the man without the woman, neither the woman without the man, in the Lord" (1 Corinthians 11:11-12).

These scriptural passages reveal some of the reasons why my good friend Keith had such a difficult time accepting the teachings of his church. Keith was a minister of a church which held as one of its fundamental tenets that marriage endured for this life only. As a legally authorized agent for his church, he performed wedding ceremonies on a regular basis, but was deeply troubled by the phrase included in his church's traditional wedding service which only allowed him to bind a man and woman until "death do you part."

As engaged couples met with Keith to discuss their marriage plans, they would often express that their love for each other was so great that they would like to be married for all eternity, not for this life only. Frustrated, Keith would reluctantly inform them that he wasn't authorized to change the traditional language of the marriage ceremony, and was obligated to grant them a marriage which automatically terminated at death. As he performed these ceremonies, he would often grieve inwardly on an occasion which should have been a joyous event.

Keith studied the Bible seriously and diligently and, consequently, he was convinced that the Lord and His apostles taught the eternal nature of marriage. As he pondered the scriptures, his heart told him that such a sacred bond given by God must be everlasting.

As a result, the concept espoused by his church that families were not eternal haunted him throughout his ministerial life. He finally reached the point where he could no longer act contrary to his innermost convictions, therefore he rewrote the wedding ceremony in accordance with his personal beliefs. Now in possession of his newly revised version of the wedding service, he was determined to marry couples for all eternity.

Although this change appealed to him on paper and sounded impressive as he conducted the actual ceremony, he was still troubled by the realization that he did not possess the proper authority to perform such an act. He could not receive it from his church, for it opposed the idea of eternal marriage. He couldn't grant it to himself, since one can only give something which he already possesses. His heart longed for this authority, but he didn't know how or where to obtain it. His prayers and studies led him to believe that such special authority must only come from God. He could only hope that his Heavenly Father would honor his humble petition for additional truth and authority.

Keith's continued search for truth guided him to more treasures of spiritual knowledge on the subject of eternal marriage as he was directed by the Lord's Spirit. Unable to withhold his newfound knowledge any longer, he began to openly teach the principle of eternal families to other members of his church. When word of his actions — teaching and performing eternal marriages — reached his church board, he was summarily excommunicated from the church, severing his ties from the work he so dearly loved.

How it hurt Keith to be barred from his church, yet he realized that this was part of his Heavenly Father's plan to grant him the freedom to teach what he knew to be true. Knowing he still lacked the authority to perform eternal marriages, he persevered in his search for power and knowledge from God.

His heartfelt prayers were finally heard and answered, as the Lord sent him the missionaries from The Church of Jesus Christ of Latter-day Saints. As he listened intently to the message brought by the Lord's earthly messengers over the next several weeks, the Spirit testified to his soul that their teachings were from God. Keith shared his own knowledge of eternal families with the missionaries and was elated to learn that this was indeed a true principle of the gospel of Jesus Christ.

When Keith was baptized into the Lord's Church, he knew that his search was over; he had found where the proper priesthood authority resided to perform eternal marriages and seal generations of families together forever. Great has been his joy since finding the

Lord's restored gospel and Church.

Life's greatest joys come from the love shared by a man and a woman, whose lives and aspirations can forever become interlocked and interwoven. Latter-day Saints believe that eternal life encompasses this transcendent love. Where there is no eternal love and marriage, there is no eternal life, for they are inextricably linked together.

MARITAL LOVE VS. SIBLING LOVE

Perhaps the greatest gospel teaching to be restored by the Lord in these latter days, as part of the "restitution of all things" of which Peter spoke (Acts 3:21), concerns this principle of the eternal nature of the family. Latter-day Saints recognize the family unit as the most important organization in heaven and earth. We regard marriage and other family relationships with a special reverence, due to our belief in their potentially eternal nature. When conducted by the proper priesthood authority and in the manner prescribed by the Lord, the marriage covenant endures beyond the grave to bind man and wife together for time and all eternity. This glorious gospel principle was restored to the earth by the Lord in these last days through His chosen servant, Joseph Smith.

Latter-day Saints believe that love is as eternal as the spirit of man itself. Just as man continues after death, so, too, does love. Are we to believe that the love developed in this life between two people will perish in the grave? I am not speaking merely of brotherly or sisterly love, but of the more profound love that ideally exists between husband and wife. Anyone who has ever married knows that the love shared with their spouse is much deeper and much different than the love shared with a brother or sister.

Latter-day Saints do not believe that God would allow this more profound marital love to abide in this mortal life only to be extinguished in the next. There would be no hope for a better life in the hereafter if one was to believe that the unique love shared by husband and wife was to be replaced by an inferior sibling love. I do indeed love my brothers and sister immensely, yet this love in no way compares to the greater love that I reserve for my wife. The gospel of Jesus Christ assures us that this greater love can continue forever in the eternities.

The Church of Jesus Christ of Latter-day Saints is unique in its belief in the doctrine of eternal marriage and eternal families. The standard phraseology used in most modern marriage ceremonies includes the words "until death do you part," thus granting the newlywed couple an automatic bill of divorce before they even commence their march together down the path of life. The bride and groom are told, in effect, that upon death they will be separated and will no longer have claim upon each other. Their marriage covenant is fulfilled, completed, and, thus, dissolved, upon death. The Latter-day Saints are grateful that the restored gospel of Jesus Christ makes provision for the continuance of the marriage covenant throughout eternity, and invite all people to partake of the great blessings of this eternal principle.

Although the popular doctrine of our day teaches that matrimony ceases with death, it has been my experience that many still believe in or hope for marriages and family relationships that will survive mortal death. Many people recognize and long for the true teachings of Christ regarding marriage and family. They recognize the love they share with their spouse and children, maintaining a personal hope that this unique and special love will succeed the grave. The whisperings of the Spirit of God have revealed to them that this can be so. But what hope have they? What promise do they have that their marriage is eternal when they have been married only "until death?" What provision has been made to guarantee the extension of their marriage or family organization beyond death?

During a gospel discussion, a gentleman once assured me that any hope for an eternal marriage is merely "wishful thinking." I was surprised by his response. This was a comment I expected to hear coming from the lips of an atheist or agnostic, not from a man of faith. It is not uncommon for nonbelievers to argue that any hope for life after death is nothing more than "wishful thinking." However, to hear a man of faith proclaiming that there are limits to God's power and love is a most bewildering and discomforting experience.

Is anything too great for the Lord to accomplish? Is there any limit to God's love for His children? Why would God withhold the greatest of all gifts, the continuance of marital and other family relationships in the eternities, from His children?

The Bible and Eternal Marriage

Latter-day Saints do not depend solely on the Bible for their understanding of this principle of eternal marriage, but rely instead on modern-day revelation from the Lord. Nevertheless, the principle of eternal marriage is in harmony with biblical scripture. The Apostle Peter revealed his understanding that husband and wife would inherit eternal life together when he wrote, "Likewise, ye husbands, dwell with them according to knowledge, giving honour unto the wife, as unto the weaker vessel, and as being *heirs together of the grace of life;* that your prayers be not hindered" (1 Peter 3:7). In this scripture, Peter is speaking of eternal life, not simply mortal life, for the life we are to inherit as "joint-heirs with Christ" (Romans 8:17) is eternal life in the kingdom of God.

Paul also taught, "Nevertheless neither is the man without the woman, neither the woman without the man, *in the Lord*" (1 Corinthians 11:11). Are we not to live "in the Lord" in the hereafter, as well as in this life?

Christ Himself taught the eternal nature of marriage when He said, "For this cause shall a man leave his father and mother, and cleave to his wife; And they twain shall be one flesh: so then they are no more twain, but one flesh. *What therefore God hath joined together, let not man put asunder*" (Mark 10:7-9). When marriage is performed according to God's power and instruction, it will endure all of man's attempts to put it "asunder." While man may bind husband and wife "until death," true representatives of God, when operating in their priesthood capacity within God's holy temples, may bind them for "all eternity."

Jesus said to Peter, "And I will give unto thee the keys of the kingdom of heaven: and *whatsoever thou shalt bind on earth shall be bound in heaven:* and whatsoever thou shalt loose on earth shall be loosed in heaven" (Matthew 16:19). Among other things, Peter received the power and authority to bind husband and wife together forever.

This same binding, or sealing, power has been restored to earth in our day and is currently held by the prophet who stands as the earthly head of The Church of Jesus Christ of Latter-day Saints. The prophet delegates this God-given power and authority to righteous individuals who serve the Lord in His holy temples located throughout the world, as they seal up husbands and wives to each other for time and all eternity before sacred altars of God.

Paul wrote to the saints at Ephesus, "Wives, submit yourselves unto your own husbands, as unto the Lord. For *the husband is the head of the wife, even as Christ is the head of the church:* and he is the saviour of the body. Therefore as the church is subject unto Christ, so let the wives be to their own husbands in everything. *Husbands, love your wives, even as Christ also loved the church,* and gave himself for it" (Ephesians 5:22-25). There will never come a time when Christ will cease to be the head of the Church, not in this life nor in the life to come.[1] Nor will there ever come a time when Christ will cease to love His Church. If the husband is to lead and love his wife, even as Christ leads and loves His Church, then he must be her husband in the hereafter as well as in mortality.

After the Lord placed Adam in the Garden of Eden, He declared, "It is not good that the man should be alone; I will make him an help meet for him" (Genesis 2:18). The Lord then gave Eve to be Adam's wife, and instructed Adam to "cleave unto his wife: and they shall be one flesh" (Genesis 2:24-25). This was the first eternal marriage performed on this earth, since Adam and Eve were immortal beings at this time, not yet subject to physical death. It wasn't until after they at the fruit of the tree of knowledge of good and evil that death was introduced into the world (Genesis 2:17; 1 Corinthians 15:22). Whenever the Lord brings a man and woman together in a holy union, and the participants live up to their sacred covenants, we can rest assured that the bond is eternal, for "whatsoever God doeth, it shall be forever" (Ecclesiastes 3:14).

Surely some will question the integrity of this sacred doctrine by referring to an experience in the life of the Savior as preserved for our study in Matthew 22:23-30. In this scripture, we learn that a group of individuals belonging to the Jewish sect, known as the Sadducees, approached Christ with a question regarding marriage. According to Jewish law, if a man died, his wife was to live with his brother. In the scenario presented by the Sadducees, when a certain woman's first husband died, she went with his brother, who also died, and likewise until the seventh brother. The Sadducees asked, "Therefore in the resurrection whose wife shall she be of the seven" (Matthew 22:28)? Jesus responded, "Ye do err, not knowing the scriptures, nor the power of God. For in the resurrection they neither marry, nor are given in marriage, but are as the angels of God in heaven" (Matthew 22:30).

The key to understanding Christ's response lies in verse 23, which states that the Sadducees "say that there is no resurrection." Obviously, their question was not sincere, for they did not believe in the resurrection, much less in eternal marriage. They were attempting to confuse the Lord in hopes of revealing Him as a fraud. The Lord, detecting their real intentions, saw this as an opportunity to teach, but was careful not to "cast pearls before swine," especially considering the sacred nature of the topic.

The Lord was not about to give a complete doctrinal dissertation on the subject of eternal marriage when they were obviously spiritually unprepared to receive it. Instead, He wisely chose to answer their question commensurate with their knowledge and teachability by simply stating that "*in* the resurrection they neither marry, nor are given in marriage." In other words, eternal marriage is a gospel ordinance to be performed on earth *before* the resurrection, not *in* or *during* the resurrection. All matters of marital status must be settled before this time in order to be effective and binding in the eternities.

As for the woman in the scenario proposed by the Sadducees, if sealed to her first husband in the temple by the proper priesthood authority, she would remain his wife in the hereafter, granted they both are worthy of these glorious blessings. The remaining six brothers would be married to her during mortality only.

MODERN REVELATION AND ETERNAL MARRIAGE

Let us hear the Lord's will on this matter as revealed in these latter days: "Therefore, if a man marry him a wife in the world, and he marry her not by me nor by my word, and he covenant with her so long as he is in the world and she with him, their covenant and marriage are not of force when they are dead, and when they are out of the world; therefore, they are not bound by any law when they are out of the world.

"Therefore, when they are out of the world they neither marry nor are given in marriage; but are appointed angels in heaven, which angels are ministering servants, to minister for those who are worthy of a far more, and an exceeding, and an eternal weight of glory.

"And again, verily I say unto you, if a man marry a wife by my word, which is my law, and by the new and everlasting covenant, and it is sealed unto them by the Holy Spirit of promise, by him who is anointed, unto whom I have appointed this power and the keys of this priesthood; and it shall be said unto them — Ye shall come forth in the first resurrection; and if it be after the first resurrection, in the next resurrection; and shall inherit thrones, kingdoms, principalities, and powers, dominions, all heights and depths — then shall it be written in the Lamb's Book of Life...it shall be done unto them in all things whatsoever my servant hath put upon them, in time, and through all eternity; and shall be of full force when they are out of the world..." (D&C 132:15-16,19).

The special love that husband and wife nurture and develop throughout mortality must not necessarily come to an abrupt end. One of the greatest truths revealed to man in this age, or for that matter, in any age, is the doctrine of eternal families. If married by the power of God, by His appointed servants, according to the manner that God has prescribed, the marriage covenant will transcend the barrier that man calls death, to continue throughout all eternity. What spiritually inclined person would consciously deprive him or herself of the choice personal blessings that expand infinitely throughout eternity from this great gospel principle? This eternal principle not only gives us a more glorious life to anticipate, but it gives us greater reason to honor our family relationships in mortality as well.

9

THE DOCTRINE OF ETERNAL PROGRESSION

SOME of life's richest blessings and profoundest lessons come to us through the sacred roles of father and mother. The unique opportunities and challenges of parenting provide the medium for some of our greatest joys, as well as our deepest sorrows. Most parents would probably agree that few things compare to the joy of watching their children grow up, advancing from year to year in their mental, physical, and emotional development.

As the father of seven exuberant children, I can honestly say that my emotions and feelings have intensified in ways I never imagined as a result of my child-rearing experiences. My personal weaknesses of impatience, frustration, disappointment, and anger have been tested and tempered, while my feelings of joy, love, charity, and compassion have grown to new and previously unknown bounds. I can attest unequivocally that I have discovered aspects of my inner self that I never knew existed, owing to my experience as a father. My soul has been stretched; my ideals and aspirations have risen to loftier heights.

The personal experiences I have thus far shared with my children have served to foster a deep, abiding love for them and forge an unbreakable bond with each of them. My ever-increasing love for them has instilled within me a desire to provide them with all the blessings of life I have come to enjoy and cherish. Like most other parents, I am willing to sacrifice all that I have for their happiness and well-being, thereby ensuring that they fulfill the divine measure of their creation. Undoubtedly, there are parents who stifle the mental, physical, emotional, or spiritual development of their children, but it is difficult to imagine any parent doing so deliberately.

One of the greatest examples of sacrifice made by a father or mother which has come to my attention, occurred in the family of a good friend. My friend grew up in a fairly large city as the youngest of five sons and one daughter, all of whom were active, energetic, and creative children. The parents quickly learned that if they did not properly channel the raw energy of their five sons, then these boys would inevitably find their own outlets to expend their seemingly inexhaustible reserves. Their father realized that each was a rough stone in need of refinement and polish.

After my friend's oldest brother became involved in drugs, his father knew that he couldn't stand to see another of his precious children tempted by the entrapments of the world. He needed to establish a strategy to provide his irrepressible boys the means whereby they could unleash their physical energy and develop their character and spiritual qualities at the same time. As he pondered his predicament, he came up with the plan of plans — he would buy a farm. Not just any farm, but a rundown, ill-maintained farm in need of much work and repair.

Before the boys knew what hit them, the entire family was moving from the city to the fresh air of the open country. When the boys saw their new home, they thought their father must have lost his mind. They soon discovered that the only thing that worked on this farm was them. And work they did — from sunup to sundown, except during the school year, when they were put to work from the moment school let out. Everyday but the Sabbath, they worked to the point of exhaustion. When the work was done, these imaginative kids discovered that the farm also offered endless opportunities for recreation.

Each morning their father would descend from the top of the tall red barn whose roof was in desperate need of repair. Although he sported a carpenter's belt full of nails and a large hammer, the family never heard any pounding while he was on the roof. Despite his big city upbringing in Detroit, Michigan, without one single day of farming experience in his entire life, their father always seemed to have the remarkable insight and inspiration required to know exactly what to do on the farm after spending a little time on the roof. The boys were convinced that the old red barn roof served as a personal "Mt. Sinai" for their father.

If he wasn't patching the roof, then what was their father doing up there? He was fulfilling another part of his master plan to keep his boys busy. They were unaware that he would observe the neighboring farms to see what the other farmers were doing that particular week. If they were plowing the ground, he would come down from the roof and announce, "Boys, fire up the tractor! It's time to plow the fields!" They never ceased to be amazed that the "Farmer on the Roof," as they would call their father, always knew what to do next.

After weeks of hard work, the fields were plowed, seeds were planted, and a hearty crop began to grow. At last, the father decided the repair of the barn roof could no longer be delayed. As the boys reached the top of the barn with their own carpenter belts, they were astonished that they could see all the neighboring farms for miles around. And they could see with great clarity exactly what the other farmers were doing and how they accomplished their tasks. It was no coincidence that the neighboring farmers were also repairing their barn roofs on that particular day.

As this dedicated father worked with his sons, he would find opportunities to spend individual time with each one to teach them timeless lessons and assist them in setting lifelong goals. He took each one aside at the appropriate time in their lives, and said, "Son, what you do with your life is your business, but there are just six things that I would like for you to do. First, get your Duty to God Award (an achievement award indicating the child has met certain standards of Christ-like behavior). Second, graduate from seminary (a four-year curriculum designed for high school-aged youth which uses the scriptures as its text). Third, get your Eagle Scout award. Fourth, go on a church mission. Fifth, get a good college education. Sixth, get married in the temple." He did the same with his daughter, helping her to set suitable lifelong goals.

As evidence of the blessings of what involved parents can accomplish, each of this father's sons and daughter to whom he issued the challenge achieved all these goals and are currently leading happy and productive lives. When this devoted father bought an old farm, he wasn't interested in raising crops — he was raising boys. When the last boy left home to go on a mission, his father sold the farm.

This wise father understood his sacred responsibility to help his sons and daughter fulfill their destiny and return to their Heavenly Father. His love for God and his children was so great, he was prepared to do anything to help them grow and achieve their divine potential. They were misguided youth with unlimited energy in need of a little direction, and their father took his sacred steward-ship to heart by providing that direction. He wanted to develop their character, build their self-worth, and ultimately give them all that he had and more.

Not unlike this loving father, I, too, would like to see my chil-dren fulfill their potential, surpassing me in knowledge, prosperity, joy, spirituality, righteousness, and all that is good. I want them to have a life that exceeds, or at least equals, the one that I currently enjoy. I want them to experience the best education, adequate material wealth and comforts, the happiness of a good family life, marriage to a loving spouse, freedom and opportunity to grow, and all the wonderful things that life has to offer. I anxiously anticipate the day when they will become my peers, that is to say, my intellectual equals, when we will be able to communicate and associate on a higher level, as adults and as true friends.

Now, if I, who am imperfect in my love and righteousness, would aspire to such things for my children, how much more would our Father in heaven aspire to greater things for His children? Isn't it conceivable that our Heavenly Father wants us to enjoy all the knowledge, abilities, capacities, happiness, and spiritual attributes that He possesses? Is there anyone who believes that we love our children more than He loves His? "If ye then, being evil, know how to give good gifts unto your children, how much more shall your Father which is in heaven give good things to them that ask him" (Matthew 7:8-11)?

As Latter-day Saints, we believe that we have a sacred obligation to assist our children in their quest to fulfill their divine potential. Like the father who raised his sons on a farm to develop their character, we have learned this great parental responsibility from our Heavenly Father who likewise desires to assist us, His children, in our eternal quest to become like Him. Through the prophet Moses, He declared, "For behold, this is my work and my glory — to bring to pass the immortality and eternal life of man" (Moses 1:39). Our Father in Heaven is the perfect parent, providing a plan whereby we may enjoy all the happiness, knowledge, and power that He currently enjoys. While my friend's father may have bought a farm for his sons, our Heavenly Father has created an entire world for us wherein we may gain invaluable experience and develop God-like qualities. By way of His condescension and grace, we may progress through the eternities until we reach that perfect day when we are like Him and are able to partake in the fulness of the blessings of His type of life, which is eternal life.

"WE ARE THE CHILDREN OF GOD"

Few beliefs or doctrines of The Church of Jesus Christ of Latter-day Saints are more misunderstood than this gospel principle of eternal progression.

Before we can fully understand this sacred principle, it is essential to preface our discussion with an examination of a few related fundamental gospel doctrines. The Bible clearly teaches that God is our Eternal Father and we are His children. Just after His death and resurrection, the Savior told Mary Magdalene, "I ascend unto my

Father, and your Father; and to my God, and your God" (John 20:17). The Apostle Paul wrote that God is the "Father of spirits" (Hebrews 12:9), meaning that we are His spirit children. He further emphasized this point when he wrote, "The Spirit itself beareth witness with our spirit, that we are the children of God" (Romans 8:16). Paul even declared that "we are the offspring of God" (Acts 17:28-29). We are more than the creatures of a Creator; we are the literal spirit children of a loving Heavenly Father.

Once we realize that we are the literal offspring of an Eternal Father, it should come as no surprise that we are spiritually begotten and physically created in His image. "And God said, Let us make man in our image, after our likeness" (Genesis 1:26). To illustrate that this "image" includes physical similarity, we learn that "Adam lived an hundred and thirty years, and begat a son in his own likeness, after his image; and called his name Seth" (Genesis 5:1-3). The likeness and image common to both Adam and Seth was also shared by God and Adam, physical likeness included. As His sons and daughters, we are made in the literal image of our Heavenly Father. When are the offspring not like the parent?

"BE YE THEREFORE PERFECT"

As the literal children of an Eternal Being in whose image we were made, we have within us the potential to become like Him. Not only do we have the opportunity to become like our Heavenly Father, we are commanded to do so. Jesus Christ issued the divine decree, "Be ye therefore perfect, even as your Father which is in heaven is perfect" (Matthew 5:48). We are to be perfect like the Father is perfect. This is no small demand. However, Christ would not ask us to do something that we could never possibly accomplish. He gave this commandment knowing full well that "with God all things are possible" (Matthew 19:26).

The word "perfect," as used in the above scriptural passage, comes from the Greek word "teleios," which has many English equivalents depending on the context in which it is used. Teleios, much like its Hebrew equivalent, tamim, can mean "morally complete or developed," "sound," "upright," "mature," "blameless," "perfect," "whole," or "full-grown."[1] One can find various examples of this usage, as in Job 1:1, "There was a man in the land of Uz, whose name was Job; and that man was perfect and upright," or in James 3:2, "If any man offend not in word, the same is a perfect man."

It can also mean "complete," "finished," "fully developed," or "having attained the appointed end of development."[2] It is in this latter context that the Savior gave the commandment to be perfect like the Father. He is commanding us to progress spiritually until we have attained to our appointed end of eternal development, which is to be fully developed "even as [our] Father which is in heaven" (Matthew 5:48).

Job was perfect as measured by certain earthly standards, however, the Savior is commanding us to become perfect according to higher, heavenly standards — a perfection which can only be totally achieved in the hereafter. The Savior exhorts us to become complete or fully developed like the Father in character, knowledge, righteousness, and in virtually all spiritual attributes. We are admonished to strive for spiritual perfection in order that we can someday, in the eternities to come, be like our Heavenly Father. The children can become like the parent, for "now are we the sons of God, and it doth not yet appear what we shall be: but we know that, when he shall appear, *we shall be like him;* for we shall see him as he is" (1 John 3:2).

Latter-day Saints do not teach that man is perfect in his current mortal state, but that he has the seeds of perfection or godhood within him. Men and women are gods and goddesses in embryo, possessing the potential to overcome their sins and weaknesses, gradually advancing "from glory to glory" (2 Corinthians 3:18), thereby ultimately becoming like their Father in heaven. That is why the Savior taught, "The kingdom of God is within you" (Luke 17:21), and Peter wrote that we "might be partakers of the divine nature" (2 Peter 1:4).

In His intercessory prayer, the Savior prayed to the Father that His disciples might attain to the same level of perfection and oneness that the members of the Godhead enjoyed. "Neither pray I for these [disciples] alone, but for them also which shall believe on me through their word;

"That they all may be one; as thou, Father, [art] in me, and I in thee, that they also may be one in us: that the world may believe that thou hast sent me.

"And the glory which thou gavest me I have given them; that they may be one, even as we are one:

"I in them, and thou in me, that *they may be made perfect* in one; and that the world may know that thou hast sent me, and hast loved them, as thou hast loved me" (John 17:20-23). Through the power of the atonement, we may be made one with the Father and the Son, and in the process, we "may be made perfect" "even as [our] Father which is in heaven is perfect."

MAN'S ETERNAL POTENTIAL

Who is to say what limits restrain the children of an omnipotent and omniscient Being? With God and His angels as our guides and teachers, the vast universe as our field of operations, and an eternity to grow and learn, who can begin to comprehend our potential for further development? What new things will our Heavenly Father teach us and what new powers will He endow us with as we abide with Him in His celestial kingdom throughout the eternities? What will be our exalted status even a billion years from now? Given the present limitations of our earthly home and mortal bodies, would not the eternal knowledge and glory to which we would attain in our Father's kingdom seem godlike in comparison?

Consider the growth or advancement of man during his brief time on earth. Within a meager 70-year life span, man is able to progress from an impotent newborn babe, initially unable to walk, talk, understand, reason, or even sustain himself, to a being that is able to split the minutest atoms, send rockets into space, harness the power of raging rivers, design complex computer systems, chart distant galaxies, and even prolong human life. Given God's assistance, man is able to rise from his ignorance and weakness, bridling some of the universe's greatest powers and discovering some of its profoundest secrets. A helpless child is able to develop the wisdom, abilities, powers, and talents, to compose the symphonies of a Mozart, formulate the scientific theorems of an Einstein, write the poetic verse of a Shakespeare, cultivate the political genius of a Madison, or attain the inspiring leadership stature of a Moses.

If man is capable of these achievements while operating within the limits of his fleeting mortal days, and removed from God's direct presence, imagine what he can accomplish or become in the eternities as a resurrected being residing in the heavens, while under the direct tutelage of Almighty God and with the resources of the celestial kingdom at his disposal. Perhaps this is why C.S. Lewis, a man much admired by modern Christians for his inspiring writings, once said, "We live in a society of possible gods and goddesses."[3]

GOD'S INFINITE LOVE AND ALMIGHTY POWER

To deny man's potential to become like his Heavenly Father is to deny God's love and power. Who would dare deny that God loves His spiritual children more than mortal parents love their own earthly children? Any loving parent would want his or her children to possess all that he or she enjoys. What good father wouldn't want his child to attain to his own knowledge and stature? As stated earlier, if I, an imperfect man, would have such lofty aspirations for my children, how much more would our perfect Father in heaven desire these things for His own children? To quote Matthew once again, "If ye then, being evil, know how to give good gifts unto your children, how much more shall your Father which is in heaven give good things to them that ask him" (Matthew 7:8-11)?

Heavenly Father's love for us is so great that He wants us to enjoy all the knowledge, joy, power, and glory, that He currently enjoys, for this is eternal life. Eternal life is God's life. If we are worthy to attain to eternal life, we will enjoy the life that our Heavenly Father enjoys, along with all its associated benefits and blessings. *"He that overcometh shall inherit all things; and I will be his God, and he shall be my son"* (Revelation 21:7). Would not all the knowledge and power that God possesses be included in a celestial inheritance of "all things?"

Assuming that our loving Heavenly Father would want us to enjoy all that He enjoys, we must next consider the matter of His omnipotence. "Is anything too hard for the Lord" (Genesis 18:14)? Who would deny that God has the power to do anything? If God loves His children enough to desire that they become like Him in all his divine attributes and powers, wouldn't He possess the power to bring this to pass? Not only does our Heavenly Father want us to know what He knows, experience joy as He does, and be able to do all things that He can do, but it is also within His power to grant us these blessings. God has the power to render us omnipotent and omniscient. Essentially, to deny that we can become like our Heavenly Father in every way is to deny His infinite love and almighty power.

Heavenly Father's plan for our eternal progression makes more sense when we consider the alternative. Some would have us believe that our spiritual growth ceases with death, and that the eternities offer nothing in the way of personal development. They envision a dead-end street where the path of progression comes to an abrupt halt. Are we to believe that we will not grow, learn, or progress in the life to come? If we are allowed to progress, at what point will our progression be stopped? Will a loving Father withhold His infinite power and knowledge from us, forcing us to remain forever in our ignorance and weakness? Would He purposely restrict rather than encourage our spiritual and intellectual development when He possesses the power to nurture it? What exactly are we to do for an eternity?

THE EXAMPLE OF JESUS CHRIST

Let us look to the life of Jesus Christ as the perfect example of the path that we can follow to our Father's kingdom. The Savior was the firstborn among our Father's spirit children (Romans 8:29; Hebrews 1:6); He is our elder brother. His Father is our Father (John 20:17), making us all part of the same eternal family. He was born into this world as a baby of flesh and blood, just as all of God's children are brought into mortality. And, like many of God's children, "Jesus increased in wisdom and stature, and in favour with God and man" (Luke 2:52), and "learned he obedience by the things which he suffered" (Hebrews 5:8). In other words, the Savior did not possess all knowledge from the start, but had to grow "in wisdom" and "learn" like each of us.

Nor did Christ possess all power from the start. The scriptures teach us that Christ came into this world "a little lower than the angels" (Hebrews 2:9; Psalms 8:5). (Actually, the Hebrew text of Psalms 8:5 reads, "For thou has made him a little less than the gods"). Due to His righteousness and obedience to the Father, Christ was able to overcome all things, now sitting on the right hand of the Father where "all the angels of God worship him" (Hebrews 1:1-6). It wasn't until after His resurrection that the Savior proclaimed, "All power is *given* unto me in heaven and in earth" (Matthew 28:18). The fact that He was "given" power indicates that there must have been a time when He did not possess certain powers. However, upon the completion of His earthly mission, the Eternal Father endowed His Son with all powers pertaining to the full stature of godhood. "Worthy is the Lamb that was slain to *receive* power, and riches, and wisdom, and strength, and honour, and glory, and blessing. And every creature which is in heaven, and on the earth, and under the earth, and such as are in the sea, and all that are in them, heard I saying, *Blessing, and honour, and glory, and power, be unto him that sitteth upon the throne,* and unto the Lamb for ever and ever" (Revelation 5:12-13).

Jesus Christ was a man of flesh and blood. He was subjected to the challenges and temptations of mortality that we now face. He passed His mortal days on this dusty planet and died as all mankind must, yet He now abides in His Father's kingdom as a perfect, immortal, resurrected man. Although He was the only totally perfect and sinless man ever to live on this earth, Christ was ultimately "made perfect," in the sense that the Father is perfect, through His sufferings and trials (Hebrews 2:10; 5:8-9; 7:28).

The fact that Christ did not enjoy the same level of perfection as the Father while in mortality is evidenced by His statement, "The Father is greater than I" (John 14:28). However, anticipating a future endowment of glory, He told the Pharisees, "The third day I shall be perfected" (Luke 13:32), thus referring to the condition of complete perfection to which He would attain only after His resurrection. Due to His obedience to the Father, He now enjoys all that His Father has to give and all that godhood has to offer. Clearly, Christ progressed in wisdom and power until He achieved total perfection in our Heavenly Father's kingdom. He is our example; He is living proof that man can become as God. He, who is both God and man, now extends His hand to us saying, "Come, follow me."

EARLY CHRISTIANS AND ETERNAL PROGRESSION

The early Christians were quite familiar with this principle of eternal progression. They understood that through His atonement, Christ paved the way for us to become like Him, as was clearly taught by His apostles and subsequently by many of the early Church Fathers. This principle is hardly unique to LDS teachings, for the early Christian Church writings are rich in this doctrine of eternal progression. Once again, we see one more example of a gospel doctrine which was lost during the spiritual famine of the Dark Ages.

Consider a sampling of the writings of a few highly reputable early Church scholars. Clement of Alexandria, the second-century Christian scholar, wrote, "The Logos (Word) of God had become man so that you might learn from a man how a man may become God."[4] The second-century Church bishop, Irenaeus, asked the rhetorical question, "And how shall man pass into God if God had not been caused to pass into man?"[5] One of the premiere scholars of the early Church, Origen, encouraged his readers to "flee with all our power from being men and make haste to become gods."[6] He also taught that "from Him [Christ] there began the union of the divine with the human nature, in order that the human, by communion with the divine, might rise to be divine."[7]

Basil, who succeeded Eusebius as bishop of Caesarea[8] in the fourth century, taught that the Holy Spirit can assist us in "being made like to God — and highest of all, being made God."[9] Gregory of Nazianus, a fourth-century theologian, wrote, "I may become God to the same extent as He became man."[10] Athanasius, another fourth-century bishop, taught that the Son of God "assumed humanity that we might become God."[11] Thomas Aquinas, in promoting this concept of man's spiritual progression, quoted an earlier Christian writer, namely Augustine, thus offering perhaps the most concise and powerful statement on this great and sacred principle: "God became man, that man might become God."[12]

In reading the statements of the earliest Christian leaders and scholars, it becomes readily apparent that Joseph Smith, as an instrument in God's hands, simply restored what the early Christians already knew: that Christ became a mortal man in order that mortal man may become like Christ. And to become like Christ is to become like the Father.

THE THRONE OF GOD

Each of us, as children of our Heavenly Father, has the opportunity to overcome sin and death through the power of the Savior's atoning sacrifice. As we repent of our sins, take upon ourselves the name of Jesus Christ, and strive to obey His commandments, His grace will be sufficient to lift us from our lowly state to the heights of eternal glory that await us in the kingdom of our Heavenly Father. Jesus Christ has promised, "To him that overcometh will I grant to *sit with me in my throne, even as I also overcame, and am set down with my Father in his throne*" (Revelation 3:21). Who can begin to comprehend the limitless joy, knowledge, and powers that are associated with such a promise?

In Revelation 5:12-13, we already learned that the Savior received all blessings, honor, glory, wisdom, riches, and power when He earned the right to sit in the throne on the right hand of His Father. Now He is extending the same opportunity to each of us if we are but worthy. He is offering us a seat in His exalted throne. "The Spirit itself beareth witness with our spirit, that *we are the children of God: And if children, then heirs; heirs of God, and joint-heirs with Christ*; if so be that we suffer with him, that *we may be also glorified together*" (Romans 8:16-17). We are joint-heirs with the almighty Lord. The power and glory we can receive in the kingdom of our Father is identical to that received by our elder brother, Jesus Christ. Who can doubt the infinite knowledge, power, joy, privileges, and blessings that the Savior presently enjoys as He sits upon the right hand of God in His exalted throne reigning in righteousness over eternal kingdoms, dominions, and principalities. This is godhood; this is eternal life.

What does it mean to sit in the exalted throne of the Lord Jesus Christ? The term "throne," translated from the Greek word "thronos," is rich in symbolism and meaning. The throne is a seat of honor reserved for royalty, therefore it represents kingly power and authority.[13] According to one source, it "conveys ideas of kingship, dominion, and authority," and "the authority to reign commences on ascension to the throne."[14] When attributed to Christ, this exalted position implies the divine kingship, divine power, and divine authority that is associated with godhood. In another source we read, "Jesus also shares the Father's throne, a fact that establishes his deity."[15] Keeping in mind this symbolism of Christ's throne, when He admonishes us, "Sit with me in my throne," He means nothing less than for His faithful followers to attain to the same divine power, dominion, and authority to which He Himself has attained.

"YE ARE GODS"

The Savior clearly taught that as sons and daughters of God, we are gods and goddesses ourselves, albeit each of us is still a work in progress. When He declared His divine Sonship before the doubting Jews, they threatened to stone Him, saying, "For a good work we stone thee not; but for blasphemy; and because that thou, *being a man, makest thyself God*" (John 10:33). Jesus then responded, "Is it not written in your law, I said, *Ye are gods?* If he called them gods, unto whom the word of God came, and the scripture cannot be broken; Say ye of him, whom the Father hath sanctified, and sent into the world, Thou blasphemest; because I said, I am the Son of God?" (John 10:34-36). In other words, Christ was saying, "Why do you accuse me of blaspheming because I say that I am the Son of God, when the scriptures already declare that you are all gods and goddesses, being sons and daughters of God."

The Savior alluded to another scripture when He said, "Is it not written in your law, I said, Ye are gods?" (John 10:34). Most likely, He was making reference to Psalm 82 of the Old Testament, a scripture with which the learned Jews were all familiar. "God standeth in the congregation of the mighty; he judgeth among the gods...I have said, *Ye are gods; and all of you are children of the most High*" (Psalms 82:1,6). Through the instrumentality of this inspired psalmist, it had already been revealed to the Jews that all of God's children are gods, making the Father the "God of gods, and Lord of lords" (Deuteronomy 10:17; Psalms 136:1-3).

Admittedly, we are far from enjoying the perfection that is associated with true godhood, such as the Father enjoys, but we do possess the potential to develop beyond our embryonic state to the full stature of godhood at some future point in the eons of time to come. As children of a perfect Heavenly Father, we can begin to develop the seeds of divinity within us right now through our constant efforts to live righteously while petitioning our Father in fervent prayer for His assistance.

To those who might be startled by this seemingly new gospel teaching, it is important to keep in mind that this sacred principle was taught by the Savior and His divinely chosen prophets and apostles, as the preceding biblical references amply illustrate. The Father is not offended by His children wanting to become like Him. He is not opposed to sharing His knowledge or power with His children who humbly seek Him. Just as a good earthly father wants his child to develop and grow, becoming more like him in wisdom and understanding each day, our Heavenly Father also wants us to develop to the extent that we are like Him. Only then can we experience the fullness of joy that He enjoys.

Not only does our Father want us to develop to perfection, but He has provided the way, that is, the gospel of Jesus Christ. Through Christ's atoning sacrifice and our obedience, we can become like our Father in heaven. God is not threatened by His children growing in knowledge or power, nor does He selfishly guard His knowledge and power from His righteous children. Just as nothing would make an earthly father happier than to see his child grow, so it is with our Heavenly Father.

No righteous father would feel threatened or angry by his adoring child's humble exclamation, "I want to be like my father." Latter-day Saints feel that this is the ultimate in true worship — to aspire to be like our Heavenly Father. We glorify and praise the Father in our efforts to emulate Him, just as our Savior did. It pleases, not angers, our Father when we strive to live a Christ-like life and harbor a Christ-like attitude. That should be our greatest spiritual goal — to be Christ-like, or, in other words, to be God-like.

"THE MAN IS BECOME AS ONE OF US"

Certain biblical scriptures have led to some modern-day misunderstanding of this Christian doctrine, such as the passages in the Book of Genesis dealing with Satan's temptation of Eve in the Garden of Eden. While attempting to persuade Eve to partake of the forbidden fruit, Satan declared, "For God doth know that in the day ye eat thereof, then your eyes shall be opened, and *ye shall be as gods, knowing good and evil*" (Genesis 3:5). Since this statement was made by Satan, some have surmised that becoming like our Heavenly Father is unachievable or undesirable, perhaps even unholy. As so often is the case, Satan attempted to deceive Eve by mixing truth with error. The real deceit lies in his statement, "Ye shall not surely die" (Genesis 3:4). However, Satan was correct in saying that, as partakers of the forbidden fruit, Adam and Eve would be as God knowing good and evil. The truthfulness of this particular statement was confirmed by God's own declaration: "And the Lord God said, Behold, *the man is become as one of us, to know good and evil*" (Genesis 3:22).

Knowledge is power, and righteous application of knowledge leads to godly power. Just as Adam and Eve learned the difference between good and evil, we, too, inherited that knowledge. It is up to us to determine how we will use that knowledge and its intrinsic power. If we employ our earthly sojourn to do that which is good in the sight of God, exercising faith in Christ, and serving and loving our fellowman, then we will inherit a place in our Father's kingdom where our knowledge and righteous power can be put to even greater use. If we choose to follow a course of wickedness and disobedience, then we forfeit our heavenly inheritance and its associated joy and power.

I know that God lives and that He is the literal Father of our spirits. He has placed us here on earth as part of our eternal development in order that our true nature can be determined, whether it be good or evil, while passing our mortal days in this proving ground. Those of us that correctly choose the path of righteousness and obedience will gain the opportunity to develop until we become "perfect even as [our] Father which is in heaven is perfect" (Matthew 5:48). "Then shall the righteous shine forth as the sun in the kingdom of their Father" (Matthew 13:43). All joy, power, knowledge, glory, blessings, and honor, will be within our grasp due to the infinite love, grace, and power of our Eternal Father. I sincerely hope that you will ponder these things in your heart as you humbly petition your Father in prayer to learn of their truthfulness in order that you might sit with Christ in His throne on the right hand of the Father in the celestial mansions awaiting us on high.

10

Why I Am a Latter-day Saint

It has been approximately 17 years since I joined the LDS Church, and my faith and conviction that this is Christ's restored Church is stronger today than it has ever been. Time and space do not permit me to adequately express all the blessings my family and I have received as a result of our membership in the Lord's Church, but perhaps I can share a few of the most precious and important.

It is difficult for me to articulate the extreme happiness and peace of mind that I enjoy, knowing the purpose of life and the plan of salvation, as well as understanding my relationship to my Heavenly Father and my Savior, Jesus Christ. It is wonderful to belong to a Church that is led by living prophets and apostles who can guide us through perilous times, especially in an age when people are wandering through life without a spiritual compass. I am thankful to hold the priesthood of God — the same priesthood held by all the ancient prophets and apostles — which allows me to receive revelation for my family and bless my family members and friends in time of need.

Perhaps I can share one particular experience in which I was able to use the priesthood as an instrument in the hand of God to heal one of my children. While I was attending graduate school at Brigham Young University, my wife and I were blessed with the birth of our second child. For various personal reasons, we decided to have a home birth with a midwife rather than the normal hospital delivery. What a marvelous experience it was to witness and participate in the birth of my second child. The midwives were gentle and competent, as they coached my wife through the labor process. The delivery went as well as my wife and I had hoped it would, and we were soon holding our new baby girl in our arms.

The next day our midwife dropped by our apartment to give the baby its first well-baby checkup. As she checked the baby's heartbeat with a stethoscope, I could tell by her serious expression that something was very wrong. After several minutes and several recounts, she finally removed the stethoscope from the baby's chest and informed us that her heart was beating slow and irregularly. She even thought at one point that her heart was going to stop altogether. The baby was asleep, which would produce a slower heart rate, however, her heart should have been beating 120-160 times per minute rather than the 50-60 times it was currently beating. As my wife and I looked at each other, we were speechless. What could be wrong with our new baby girl?

My wife and I maintained a faith in our Heavenly Father, yet we were still very afraid for the well-being of our new child. After some discussion with the midwife, we agreed to take the baby to the emergency ward of the local hospital, but before we did I felt inspired to give her a priesthood blessing. Holding my newborn babe in my arms, by the authority of the priesthood of God which I rightfully held, and in the name of Jesus Christ, I called upon the powers of heaven to bless our baby with strength and good health. Then the emotions of the moment overwhelmed me as tears coursed down my cheeks, preventing me from saying anything for at least 15 seconds. I then gathered myself and concluded the blessing with a heartfelt and emotional appeal to our Heavenly Father to protect this little child from any harm. It was a very touching moment as my wife and I embraced one another and our child after the blessing. The strong presence of the Holy Ghost made us feel as though we were all being embraced by our Heavenly Father.

After our embrace, the midwife rechecked the baby's heartbeat. A miracle had occurred before our very eyes, as her heart was now beating strongly and in perfect rhythm. As a precaution, we took her to the hospital to have her checked by a doctor, who after close examination informed us that our baby girl was perfectly healthy. To our great joy, she revealed no signs of an abnormal heart rate. The doctor said that for a moment her heart seemed to slow a little, but then it picked right back up again and continued to beat normally. Today, our little baby is a healthy and active ten-year old girl, whose daredevil antics often manage to make her parents' hearts skip a few beats.

As for other blessings which derive from LDS Church membership, I have great inner peace knowing that my marriage and other family relationships are eternal, our family having been sealed together in the temple of the Lord. Great blessings also come from my extended Church family via service and fellowshipping among the Latter-day Saints, as we all work together to build the Lord's kingdom as well as build up one another.

I was once asked by a friend who was a member of another faith what I would miss the most if I left the LDS Church today. After some thought, I responded that I would miss the constant companionship of the Holy Ghost that was granted to me when worthy priesthood holders laid their hands upon my head and confirmed me a member of the Church of Jesus Christ after my baptism. Those who receive the gift of the Holy Ghost by the laying on of hands are promised that they may have the privilege of the Spirit's guidance, comfort, and protection at all times if they remain worthy of his companionship. I have a firsthand witness of the invaluable influence of the Holy Ghost in my daily life as I endeavor to follow the Savior and lead my family back to our Heavenly Father's kingdom.

The opportunity for personal revelation was especially helpful in making a pivotal decision in my life. Shortly after I returned home from my mission in France, I met a beautiful, young lady at Church that I found most captivating. After three or four weeks of dating, I asked her to marry me. She subjected me to ten minutes of nervous laughter, then replied by saying that she would pray about it.

We both thought her idea to pray for God's approval of our decision was a good one, therefore, we agreed to fast and pray for an answer. Two weeks later, we still had not sought the Lord's approval, and I began to feel an uneasiness and irritability that caused me great concern. I felt the Spirit of the Lord withdrawing from me.

I called my prospective mate to share my feelings and she informed me that she was experiencing similar feelings of anxiety. We agreed that we had procrastinated long enough; it was time to fast and pray to the Lord about our engagement plans. We felt that this was the Lord's way of telling us that he wanted us to seek his guidance in this matter now.

We began our fast on that day and closed it with prayer 24 hours later. We both knelt in prayer in my mother's home with the purpose of involving our Heavenly Father in this critical decision-making process. Having laid out our plans to marry before God, we then waited in silence with bowed heads, listening with our hearts and our minds for a response. As we continued to wait in quiet anticipation for the Lord's answer, it finally came. He spoke to us as He has spoken to His children that seek His guidance throughout the ages — by the power of the Holy Ghost.

His response was so subtle that we didn't fully understand it until long after we concluded our prayer. The anxiety and irritability we had felt during the previous several days was now conspicuously gone. A very noticeable change had taken place within each of us. By speaking peace to our very souls, the Lord had given us His divine acceptance of our marital plans. If we were still unsure by the end of our prayer, all doubt was erased from our minds within the next few days, as we continued to pray and ponder. When seeking the Lord's will on a matter, His Spirit, as our constant companion, can grant us personal assurance. "Did I not speak peace to your mind concerning the matter? What greater witness can you have than from God?" (D&C 6:23).

Another example will serve to further demonstrate the blessings we may obtain through the constant companionship of God's Spirit. No one is too young or too old to receive inspiration or comfort from God. While I was still single and living in California, a young LDS couple I met shortly after my baptism shared a wonderful spiritual experience with me which involved their little girl.

One Sunday, as they returned home from Church, they could tell something was bothering their young daughter, who was three or four years old at the time. Rather than being her bubbly and cheerful self, she was quiet and despondent. When they asked her why she was so sad, she informed them that two boys in her Primary class (Sunday School for young children) had been teasing her and told her that she was ugly. Try as they may to convince her that she was not ugly, she would not be consoled.

Her parents then told her that she should go to her room and ask her Heavenly Father to help her be happy. Begrudgingly, she climbed the stairs leading to her bedroom to say her personal prayers. Several minutes later she came down the stairs just as despondent as before. Not too encouraged by what they saw, her parents asked her how she felt. She responded, "I'm still ugly."

Not really sure what to do, they admonished her to try again and this time to keep praying until she received an answer. Surprisingly, she agreed to try one more time. Once again, she made the long climb up the stairs to retire to her room for solitude. Her parents waited anxiously below as she kneeled by her bed, pouring her fragile little heart out to her Heavenly Father.

Finally, she descended the stairs to the living room, this time her parents detecting something quite different about her. As she approached them, they could see that she now had a bounce in her step and a smile on her face. Her parents couldn't wait to ask, "Well, how did it go?"

She answered with a lively sparkle in her eyes, "Heavenly Father says I'm not ugly. He says I'm beautiful."

Who can doubt that this innocent little child had communed with her Father in Heaven? In the eternal worlds on high, God Almighty heard the heartfelt pleas of a little girl — one of His literal spirit children — and He graciously condescended to mend her broken heart as only He knows how. God truly hears our sincere prayers and comforts us when we humbly seek Him. Such are the blessings of the constant companionship of the Holy Ghost that come to faithful members of the Lord's Church.

WHY I BELIEVE IN LDS DOCTRINE

Having discussed the spiritual blessings that come from church membership, in addition to several key doctrinal issues which serve to explain LDS beliefs from a scriptural perspective, it is my sincere hope that the reasons for my conversion have become a little more apparent. To summarize the preceding chapters:

- I believe in the gospel of Jesus Christ as embraced by The Church of Jesus Christ of Latter-day Saints because it teaches, as does the Bible, that God, the Father; His Son, Jesus Christ; and the Holy Ghost, are three separate and distinct personages who are one in purpose, not in substance.

- I am a Latter-day Saint because the LDS Church teaches that our Heavenly Father, in whose image and likeness man was made, has a tangible body of flesh and bone, and is not an immaterial, ethereal essence that fills the universe.

- I am a Latter-day Saint because the LDS Church teaches that all mankind will be resurrected by virtue of the grace of God and that God will grant eternal life in His glorious kingdom to all those who believe in Jesus Christ and obey His commandments, not to those who merely pay lip service.

- I am a Latter-day Saint because the LDS Church teaches that the heavens are open and that God currently makes His will known to man by way of divine revelation as received by living prophets, while discarding the belief that the heavens are closed and God has not spoken for nearly 2,000 years.

- I am a Latter-day Saint because the LDS Church teaches that the Book of Mormon is the word of God, as is the Bible, these two volumes of holy scripture serving as sacred witnesses from two different hemispheres as to the divine mission of Jesus Christ, rather than insisting that God's wisdom and knowledge are limited to one volume of scripture.

- I am a Latter-day Saint because the LDS Church teaches that marriage and family relationships are indeed eternal when consummated and sealed by the power of God's holy priesthood and conducted in His holy temples, while dismissing the belief that marital love and family unity perish in the grave.

- I am a Latter-day Saint because the LDS Church teaches that man is the literal spirit offspring of the Father, and through the atonement of Jesus Christ, we may become like Him in divine knowledge and power and in virtually all His godly attributes — that is, we may become Christlike — rather than remain forever in a state of relative ignorance and weakness.

OTHER LATTER-DAY SAINT BELIEFS AND PRACTICES

In addition to the above-mentioned doctrinal points, the following characteristics, features, doctrines, and practices serve as further evidence of the Savior's restored Church.

PRIESTHOOD AUTHORITY

Along with the restoration of the fullness of the true gospel upon the earth, the power and authority to act in behalf of the Lord has likewise been restored, that is, the holy priesthood of God. This God-given authority consists of two divisions: the Melchizedek Priesthood and the Aaronic (or Levitical) Priesthood (Psalm 110:4; Hebrews 5:6; 7:1-28; 8:6; 1 Peter 2:9). This priesthood power and authority, along with the accompanying knowledge necessary to sufficiently comprehend its significance, function, duties, and role in the plan of salvation, has been restored via modern revelation. The keys to this power and authority are vested in he who stands as the Lord's appointed mouthpiece and earthly administrator, that is, the living prophet of The Church of Jesus Christ of Latter-day Saints.

PRIESTHOOD ORGANIZATION AND OFFICES

As previously stated, the Savior established a church, that is, an organization comprised of His true disciples, the foundation of which consisted of apostles and prophets (Ephesians 2:20; 4:11). This divinely established Church also included high priests (Hebrews 3:1; 5:1,10; 7:26), bishops (Philippians 1:1; 1 Timothy 3:1; Titus 1:7), seventies (Luke 10:1,17), elders (Acts 14:23; 20:17; Titus 1:5; 1 Peter 5:1; James 5:14), deacons (Philippians 1:1; 1 Timothy 3:8), and teachers (Ephesians 4:11), among others. All these priesthood offices, having served as vital components in the Savior's early Church (see 1 Corinthians 12), can also be found in His restored Church, The Church of Jesus Christ of Latter-day Saints.

GOSPEL ORDINANCES

Gospel ordinances such as baptism (John 3:5; Mark 16:15-16; Luke 7:29-30), laying on of hands for receiving the holy priesthood and the gift of the Holy Ghost (Acts 13:1-3; 8:14-17; 19:1-6; 1 Timothy 4:14), and partaking of the sacrament (Matthew 26:26-27; John 6:54; Acts 2:42; 20:7; 1 Corinthians 11:26), were taught by the Savior and practiced in His early Church. Today, these and other equally important ordinances are observed in the LDS Church.

HOLY TEMPLES

Throughout the ages, God's people have erected holy houses, known as temples (2 Samuel 7:5; 1 Chronicles 22:6; Ezra 4:1; Habakkuk 2:20; Haggai 2:18; Zechariah 6:13; Malachi 3:1; Luke 24:53; Acts 2:46; 21:26-30; Revelation 7:15), wherein sacred ordinances were performed to fulfill the requirements of the Lord's prescribed manner of true worship. The sacred nature of temples in general was demonstrated by the Savior's reaction as He witnessed the defilement of the temple in Jerusalem by those who sought to employ its holy premises for worldly gain (Matthew 21:12-13; John 2:16). As He cast out the money changers in righteous indignation, He declared, "It is written, My house shall be called the house of prayer; but ye have made it a den of thieves" (Matthew 21:13).

Today, the Lord's people are still a temple-building people, serving God day and night in His holy sanctuaries. In these sacred edifices, gospel ordinances such as eternal marriage are performed, as well as vicarious work for those who have passed from this mortal existence without ever having had the opportunity to hear the gospel of Jesus Christ. Through the channel of divine revelation, latter-day prophets of Jesus Christ have received the Lord's instruction pertaining to the proper modes and procedures for temple construction and worship. All mankind is invited to partake of the eternal blessings that can only be realized in God's holy temples.

The Lord has never called an end to temple worship. In fact, the scriptures reveal the importance of continued temple worship even after the Savior's atoning sacrifice, as well as during the last days and into the Millennium.

After the death and resurrection of Jesus Christ, His apostles continued to worship and serve God in his temple on a daily basis (Acts 2:46). According to Luke, after the ascension of the resurrected Lord, His disciples "were continually in the temple, praising and blessing God" (Luke 24:53). John the Revelator received a vision of events to transpire prior to Christ's Second Coming, among which he witnessed 144,000 righteous disciples of the Lord serving him "day and night in his temple" (Revelation 7:15).

Writing of the actual time of the Lord's Second Coming, Malachi records this statement made by the Lord: "Behold, I will send my messenger, and he shall prepare the way before me: and *the Lord, whom ye seek, shall suddenly come to his temple,* even the messenger of the covenant, whom ye delight in: behold, he shall come, saith the Lord of hosts. But who may abide the day of his coming? and who shall stand when he appeareth? (Malachi 3:1-2).

It is the Latter-day Saints who are "continuing daily with one accord in the temple" (Acts 2:46). It is the Latter-day Saints who build temples to which the Lord may "suddenly come" at His appointed time. It is the Latter-day Saints who "serve him day and night in his temple," fulfilling their roles as servants in His kingdom on earth and awaiting the great day of His coming. And it is the Latter-day Saints who invite all mankind to participate in this sacred work and share in its eternal blessings.

MISSIONARY WORK

While He was still on the earth, the Savior commanded His apostles to preach the gospel to all nations and peoples and to baptize those who accepted their glorious message in the name of the Father, Son, and Holy Ghost (Matthew 24:14; 28:19; Mark 16:15). With approximately 60,000 full-time missionaries serving in over 100 nations throughout the four corners of the globe, the Latter-day Saints are going forth two by two (Luke 10:1) to labor in the Lord's vineyard to preach the gospel of Jesus Christ. The LDS Church has accepted this divine commission to preach the gospel of Jesus Christ to each and every one of our Heavenly Father's children, regardless of nationality, creed, race, or tongue. The Lord's Church is a missionary church.

LAY CLERGY

Just as early representatives of Christ's Church preached the gospel freely, receiving no wages for their labors (1 Peter 5:2; 1 Corinthians 9:18; 2 Corinthians 12:16-18; 2 Thessalonians 3:8-9), so, too, do the Lord's modern-day representatives preach without expectation of monetary gain. Local leaders such as bishops sustain themselves financially as doctors, lawyers, professors, bankers, entrepreneurs, plumbers, electricians, farmers, or in any other profession whereby men may honorably support their families. Missionaries and lay clergy leaders receive no wages for their services, spending their own precious time and resources as they serve the Lord and assist in the building of His kingdom on earth. The gospel is not to be sold at a price.

FASTING AND PRAYING

In ancient times, the Lord's disciples often fasted and prayed in order to overcome the appetites of the physical body, and thus heighten their spirituality and sensitivity to the Holy Spirit (Matthew 17:21; Luke 2:37; 18:12; Acts 13:2; 14:23; 1 Corinthians 7:5). The Latter-day Saints likewise observe this practice, fasting for a 24-hour period once a month. The money saved from the two to three forgone meals is then contributed as a fast offering to feed the poor, clothe the naked, and shelter the homeless.

ADMINISTERING TO THE SICK

Among the duties of priesthood holders is the responsibility to bless the sick and afflicted. "Is any sick among you? let him call for the elders [those holding the Melchizedek Priesthood] of the church; and let them pray over him, anointing him with oil in the name of the Lord" (James 5:14). This early Christian practice wherein priesthood holders anointed the sick with consecrated olive oil, then laid their hands upon them in order to bless them in the name of the Lord (Acts 28:8; Mark 6:5,13; 16:18) continues today in the Savior's Church.

CHRIST'S ANCIENT AND RESTORED CHURCHES: EXPECTED PARALLELS

These are but a few of the many similarities between the early Christian Church and The Church of Jesus Christ of Latter-day Saints. It should come as no surprise to find such a close parallel between these two churches, since they share a common denominator — both were established by our Lord and Savior, Jesus Christ. Hopefully, this book has sufficiently illustrated the abundant biblical support for LDS beliefs, as well as the profound consistency between the Lord's Church as revealed in the New Testament and His Church restored in these latter days.

Like His first-century Church, the Savior's restored latter-day church makes provision for apostles, prophets, high priests, bishops, seventies, elders, deacons, teachers, baptism by immersion, laying on of hands, holy temples, blessings of the sick with consecrated oil, world-wide missionary work, partaking of the sacrament, fasting and prayer, a lay clergy, spiritual gifts, the Melchizedek and

Aaronic Priesthoods, tithing, members called saints, eternal marriage, continuous revelation, and so on and so on. In His infinite goodness and wisdom, the Savior has seen fit to restore this same organization, along with all of its authority, doctrine, and practices, to prepare us for His glorious Second Coming.

I solemnly testify that The Church of Jesus Christ of Latter-day Saints is the Savior's restored Church. It represents the kingdom of God on earth possessing all the truth, power, and authority necessary to assist us in our return to our Father in Heaven. I bear witness that the current head of this Church is God's divinely appointed servant who serves as prophet, seer, and revelator for all mankind. I bear witness that Jesus Christ is the Savior of the world and that He chose Joseph Smith as His divinely commissioned instrument to restore His eternal gospel and Church to the earth in these latter days. I bear witness that the Book of Mormon is the word of God, as received by ancient American prophets through the power of the Holy Ghost, and that it joins together with the Bible as a witness to the divine mission of Jesus Christ. Above all, I testify that God lives and that He loves each and every one of us, for we are His children. May you pray to your Father in Heaven to learn the truthfulness of these things as you ponder them with an open heart and mind, for this is the purpose of life, I beseech you in the name of our Beloved Savior, even Jesus Christ.

ENDNOTES

CHAPTER 1

1. Charles W. Penrose, *Why I Am a Mormon* (Deseret News Press, Salt Lake City, Utah, 1971), pp. 1-2.

CHAPTER 2

1. Richard Lloyd Anderson, *Understanding Paul* (Deseret Book Company, Salt Lake City, Utah, 1983), p. 216.

2. James E. Talmage, *Jesus the Christ* (The Church of Jesus Christ of Latter-day Saints, Salt Lake City, Utah, 1981), p. 500.

3. J.N.D. Kelly, *Early Christian Doctrines* (Harper & Row, San Francisco, CA, 1978), p. 129.

4. Dr. Tim Dowley, *Eerdman's Handbook to the History of Christianity* (William B. Eerdmans Publishing Co., Grand Rapids, MI, 1977), p. 76, 111. J.N.D. Kelly, *Early Christian Doctrines,* (Harper & Row, San Francisco, CA, 1978), p. 113. Eugene Seaich, *Mormonism, the Dead Sea Scrolls, and the Nag Hammadi Texts* (Sounds of Zion, Midvale, Utah, 1980), p. 62.

5. J.N.D. Kelly, *Early Christian Doctrines* (Harper & Row, San Francisco, CA, 1978), p. 88.

6. Ibid., p. 271.

7. Ibid., pp. 90-137.

8. Ibid., p. 90.

9. Hugh W. Nibley, *The World and the Prophets* (Deseret Book Company, Salt Lake City, Utah, and Foundation for Ancient Research and Mormon Studies, Provo, Utah, 1987), p. 28.

10. Dr. Tim Dowley, *Eerdman's Handbook to the History of Christianity* (William B. Eerdmans Publishing Co., Grand Rapids, MI, 1977), p. 134.

11. Hugh W. Nibley, *The World and the Prophets* (Deseret Book Company, Salt Lake City, Utah, and Foundation for Ancient Research and Mormon Studies, Provo, Utah, 1987), pp. 45-46.

12. J.R. Dummelow, *A Commentary on the Holy Bible* (The MacMillan Company, New York, 1960), p. cxiii.

13. *The Pearl of Great Price,* Joseph Smith — History 1:16-17 (The Church of Jesus Christ of Latter-day Saints, Salt Lake City, Utah, 1981).

CHAPTER 3

1. Richard Lloyd Anderson, *Understanding Paul* (Deseret Book Company, Salt Lake City, Utah, 1983), p. 251.

2. Ibid., p. 202.

3. Ibid., pp. 249-50.

4. Ibid., p. 251.

5. LeGrand Richards, *A Marvelous Work and a Wonder* (Deseret Book Company, Salt Lake City, Utah, 1976), pp. 21-22.

6. Kent P. Jackson, "Early Signs of the Apostasy," *Ensign* Magazine, December 1984, p. 12.

7. William O. Nelson, "Is the LDS View of God Consistent With the Bible?," *Ensign* Magazine, July 1987, p. 57.

8. James E. Talmage, *The Great Apostasy* (Deseret Book Company, Salt Lake City, Utah, 1981), p. 105.

9. Hugh W. Nibley, "The God of the Philosophers" (Foundation for Ancient Research and Mormon Studies, Provo, Utah), pp. 2-8.

10. Truman G. Madsen, "Can God Be Pictured?" (BYU Studies, Provo, Utah, 1968), Vol. 8, Part 2, p. 125.

CHAPTER 4

1. Bruce R. McConkie, *Mormon Doctrine* (Bookcraft, Salt Lake City, Utah, 1966), pp. 338-39.

2. James E. Talmage, *The Articles of Faith* (The Church of Jesus Christ of Latter-day Saints, Salt Lake City, Utah, 1981), p. 480.

3. Joseph Fielding Smith, Jr., *Doctrinal Answers* (Bookcraft, Salt Lake City, Utah, 1959), p. 37.

4. Lenet Hadley Read, *How We Got the Bible* (Deseret Book Company, Salt Lake City, Utah, 1985), p. 31.

5. Hugh W. Nibley, *The World and the Prophets* (Deseret Book Company, Salt Lake City, Utah, and Foundation for Ancient Research and Mormon Studies, Provo, Utah, 1987), p. 30.

6. Richard Lloyd Anderson, *Understanding Paul* (Deseret Book Company, Salt Lake City, Utah, 1983), p. 259.

7. Robert E. Parson, "I Have a Question," *Ensign* Magazine, April 1986, p. 39.

8. Richard Lloyd Anderson, *Understanding Paul* (Deseret Book Company, Salt Lake City, Utah, 1983), p. 51.

9. Alfred Edersheim, *The Life and Times of Jesus the Messiah* (Longmans, Green, & Co., New York, 1907), Vol. 2, p. 787.

10. Richard Lloyd Anderson, *Understanding Paul* (Deseret Book Company, Salt Lake City, Utah, 1983), p. 359.

11. LeGrand Richards, *A Marvelous Work and a Wonder* (Deseret Book Company, Salt Lake City, Utah, 1976), p. 266.

12. Ben Wattenberg, "Moral Morass or Religious Revival?," Topeka Capital-Journal, April 18, 1991.

13. Lloyd Shearer, "Religious Populace," Intelligence Report, *Parade* Magazine, July 7, 1991, p. 8.

14. James Patterson and Peter Kim, *The Day America Told the Truth* (Prentice Hall, New York, 1991), p. 99.

15. Ibid., p. 205.

16. Ibid.

17. Ibid., p. 204.

CHAPTER 5

1. John Taylor, *The Gospel Kingdom* (Salt Lake City, Utah), p. 34.

2. Elder Orson F. Whitney, Conference Report, October 1916, pp. 55-56.

3. Hugh W. Nibley, *Since Cumorah* (Deseret Book Company, Salt Lake City, Utah, 1967), p. 37.

4. Elder Mark E. Peterson, *Ensign* Magazine, May 1978, p. 62.

5. Richard Lloyd Anderson, *Understanding Paul* (Deseret Book Company, Salt Lake City, Utah, 1983), p. 268.

6. Ibid., p. 419.

7. Hugh W. Nibley, *Mormonism and Early Christianity* (Deseret Book Company, Salt Lake City, Utah, and Foundation for Ancient Research and Mormon Studies, Provo, Utah, 1987), p. 272.

CHAPTER 6

1. James E. Talmage, *The Articles of Faith* (The Church of Jesus Christ of Latter-day Saints, Salt Lake City, Utah, 1981), p.237.

2. Lenet Hadley Read, *How We Got the Bible* (Deseret Book Company, Salt Lake City, Utah, 1985), p. 22.

3. Hugh W. Nibley, *Since Cumorah* (Deseret Book Company, Salt Lake City, Utah, 1967), p. 26.

4. Dr. Tim Dowley, *Eerdman's Handbook to the History of Christianity* (William B. Eerdmans Publishing Co., Grand Rapids, MI, 1977), pp. 94-95.

5. J.N.D. Kelly, *Early Christian Doctrines* (Harper & Row, San Francisco, CA, 1978), pp. 59-60.

6. Harry Y. Gamble, *The New Testament Canon: Its Making and Meaning* (Fortress Press, Philadelphia, PA, 1985), p. 12.

7. Ibid., p. 18.

8. Ibid., p. 66.

9. Ibid., p. 56.

10. Ibid., pp. 48-53. Dr. Tim Dowley, *Eerdman's Handbook to the History of Christianity* (William B. Eerdmans Publishing Co., Grand Rapids, MI, 1977), pp. 94-95.

11. Harry Y. Gamble, *The New Testament Canon: Its Making and Meaning* (Fortress Press, Philadelphia, PA, 1985), p. 57.

12. Ibid., p. 25.

13. Ibid., p. 33.

14. Ibid., p. 36.

15. Hugh W. Nibley, *Mormonism and Early Christianity* (Deseret Book Company, Salt Lake City, Utah, and Foundation for Ancient Research and Mormon Studies, Provo, Utah, 1987), p. 181.

16. Harry Y. Gamble, *The New Testament Canon: Its Making and Meaning* (Fortress Press, Philadelphia, PA, 1985) p. 58.

17. Ibid., p. 83.

18. James L. Barker, *Apostasy from the Divine Church* (Salt Lake City, Utah, 1960), p. 7.

19. Hugh W. Nibley, *Since Cumorah* (Deseret Book Company, Salt Lake City, Utah, 1967), pp. 118-19.

20. Ibid., p. 110.

21. Hugh W. Nibley, *Mormonism and Early Christianity* (Deseret Book Company, Salt Lake City, Utah, and Foundation for Ancient Research and Mormon Studies, Provo, Utah, 1987), p. 153.

22. J.N.D. Kelly, *Early Christian Doctrines* (Harper & Row, San Francisco, CA, 1978), p. 33.

23. Hugh W. Nibley, *The World and the Prophets* (Deseret Book Company, Salt Lake City, Utah, and Foundation for Ancient Research and Mormon Studies, Provo, Utah, 1987) p. 30.

24. Ibid.

25. Ibid., p. 65.

26. Hugh W. Nibley, *Since Cumorah* (Deseret Book Company, Salt Lake City, Utah, 1967), p. 126.

27. William Barclay, *Introducing the Bible* (Abingdon Press, Nashville, TN, 1972), pp. 133-134.

28. James L. Barker, *Apostasy from the Divine Church* (Salt Lake City, Utah, 1960), p. 14.

29. Dr. Tim Dowley, *Eerdman's Handbook to the History of Christianity* (William B. Eerdmans Publishing Co., Grand Rapids, MI, 1977), p. 92.

30. Harry Y. Gamble, *The New Testament Canon: Its Making and Meaning* (Fortress Press, Philadelphia, PA, 1985), pp. 38-39.

31. Ibid., p. 41.

32. Ibid., p. 28.

33. *Holy Bible*, Translators to the Reader, King James Version, pp. 9-17.

34. *Holy Bible,* Revised Standard Version (Thomas Nelson & Sons, New York, 1952), pp. iii-vi.

35. Ibid., p. vi.

36. *Holy Bible*, New International Version (Zondervan Bible Publishers, Grand Rapids, MI, 1978), pp. vii-x.

37. Ibid., p. viii.

38. Hugh W. Nibley, *Mormonism and Early Christianity* (Deseret Book Company, Salt Lake City, Utah, and Foundation for Ancient Research and Mormon Studies, Provo, Utah, 1987), pp. 248-50.

39. Robert J. Matthews, "I Have a Question," *Ensign* Magazine, February 1978, pp. 22-23.

40. Hugh W. Nibley, *Mormonism and Early Christianity* (Deseret Book Company, Salt Lake City, Utah, and Foundation for Ancient Research and Mormon Studies, Provo, Utah, 1987), p. 230.

41. Ibid., p. 231.

42. *Joseph Smith's "New Translation" of the Bible* (Herald Publishing House, Independence, MO, 1970), p. 127.

43. Ibid., p. 229.

44. Ibid., p. 485.

45. Ibid., p. 444.

46. Ibid., pp. 127-28.

47. Ibid., p. 121.

48. Ibid., p. 143.

49. Monte S. Nyman and Robert L. Millet, *The Joseph Smith Translation: The Restoration of Plain and Precious Things* (Religious Studies Center, Brigham Young University, Provo, Utah, 1985), pp. 36, 252.

50. *Joseph Smith's "New Translation" of the Bible* (Herald Publishing House, Independence, MO, 1970), p. 483.

51. Monte S. Nyman and Robert L. Millet, *The Joseph Smith Translation: The Restoration of Plain and Precious Things* (Religious Studies Center, Brigham Young University, Provo, Utah, 1985), p. 218.

52. Joseph Fielding Smith, *The Teachings of the Prophet Joseph Smith* (Deseret Book Company, Salt Lake City, Utah, 1976), p. 327.

53. Richard Lloyd Anderson, *Understanding Paul* (Deseret Book Company, Salt Lake City, Utah, 1983), p. 53.

54. *The Life and Teachings of Jesus & His Apostles* (The Church of Jesus Christ of Latter-day Saints, Salt Lake City, Utah, 1979), p. 215.

55. Robert J. Matthews, "I Have a Question," *Ensign* Magazine, July 1985, p. 19.

CHAPTER 7

1. Keith H. Meservy, "Ezekiel's 'Sticks'," *Ensign* Magazine, September 1977, pp. 25-26.

2. Robert J. Matthews, "I Have a Question," *Ensign* Magazine, July 1985, p. 17.

CHAPTER 8

1. LeGrand Richards, *A Marvelous Work and a Wonder* (Deseret Book Company, Salt Lake City, Utah, 1976), pp. 194-95.

CHAPTER 9

1. Paul J. Achtemeier, General Editor, *Harper's Bible Dictionary* (Harper & Row, San Francisco, 1985), p. 771. John L. McKenzie, *Dictionary of the Bible* (The Bruce Publishing Co., Milwaukee, WI, 1965), p. 659. George Arthur Buttrick, Editor, *Interpreter's Dictionary of the Bible* (Abingdon Press, New York, 1962), p. 730. G.W.Bromiley, General Editor, *The International Standard Bible Encyclopedia* (William B. Eerdmans Publishing Co., Grand Rapids, MI, 1988), pp. 764-65. J.D.Douglas, Editor, *The Illustrated Bible Dictionary* (Inter-Varsity Press, Tyndale House Publishers, Wheaton, Il, 1980), pp. 1190-91.

2. Ibid.

3. C.S. Lewis, *The Weight of Glory* (William B. Eerdmans Publishing Co., Grand Rapids, MI, 1975), p. 15.

4. *Clement of Alexandria*, Exhortation to the Greeks I.8.4.

5. Irenaeus, *Against the Heretics* IV.33.4.

6. Origen, *On the Gospel of John* 11.3,19, cf. 20.29.

7. Origen, *Against Celsus* III.28.

8. Dr. Tim Dowley, *Eerdman's Handbook to the History of Christianity* (William B. Eerdmans Publishing Co., Grand Rapids, MI, 1977), p. 66.

9. *Basil of Caesaria*, On the Holy Spirit IX.23.

10. *Gregory of Nazianus*, Orations XXIX.19.

11. *Athanasius*, On the Incarnation of the Word 65. Cf. Orations Against the Arians I.11 38-39, II,19.47.

12. Thomas Aquinas, *Summa Theologica* 3 Q.1. art 2.

13. George Arthur Buttrick, Editor, *The Interpreter's Dictionary of the Bible* (Abingdon Press, New York, 1962), Vol. 4, pp. 636-37. G.W.Bromiley, General Editor, *The International Standard Bible Encyclopedia*, (William B. Eerdmans Publishing Co., Grand Rapids, MI, 1988), pp. 844-45. *Greek Bible Lexicon on CD*, Gospel Library, Third Edition, (Infobases International Inc., 1994).

14. G.W.Bromiley, General Editor, *The International Standard Bible Encyclopedia*, (William B. Eerdmans Publishing Co., Grand Rapids, MI, 1988), p. 844.

15. *The Revell Bible Dictionary* (Fleming H. Revell Co., Old Tappan, NJ, 1984).

Biography

THE author grew up in Fresno, California, the second of three children who comprised the family's second generation of Germans from Russia to be born on American soil. The author's grandparents immigrated to the United States in 1913 and eventually ended up in California where they labored hard in the vineyards of the San Joaquin Valley in order to start a new life in this land of promise. His parents met in Fresno after his father returned from active duty in the Army during World War II, serving his country in the South Pacific theatre of the war.

Having been raised as a Lutheran, the author departed from the family's long-held religious tradition when he joined The Church of Jesus Christ of Latter-day Saints at the age of 24 in 1981. At the age of 26, he served a full-time proselyting mission for the Church in the France, Paris Mission. Upon completion of his mission, he returned to Fresno where he met his wife, Janice Kelly. After receiving his Bachelor of Science degree in Finance at Fresno State University, they moved to Provo, Utah. There Brad earned a Master of Business Administration degree at the Marriott School of Management at Brigham Young University.

Brad, Jan, and their seven children now reside in Topeka, Kansas, where Brad is employed as the Manager of Market Planning and Analysis at the corporate headquarters of Payless ShoeSource. Brad currently serves as the executive secretary and high priest instructor in the Lake Shawnee Ward of the Topeka, Kansas Stake. In the recent past, the author has served as stake mission president, stake high councilor, and second counselor to the bishop.